GIRL ATHLETE

Powerful stories from game-changing women

By JOAN NIESEN

Illustrated by GEORGIA RUCKER

downtown 🏢 bookworks

downtown bookworks

Downtown Bookworks Inc.
New York, New York
www.downtownbookworks.com

CONTENTS

GIRL ATHLETE

FOREWORD

If you're reading this book, we share a competitive spirit. I had four older brothers, so competition was pretty much a way of life for me from the time I was a kid. I set my first world record when I was 15 years old, and in 1984, when I was 17, I competed in my first Olympics in Los Angeles, California. At the time, everything felt so huge to me. I wasn't used to swimming in front of 10,000 people. I had barely gotten used to the idea that I was able to compete on such an elite level. And that was just the beginning of my journey!

Twenty-four years later, at the age of 41, I won my last three medals in my fifth Olympics. By then, I was a mom, I'd had decades of experience both in and out of the pool, and I was still able to set records. At that point, I had gone from youthful awe to gratitude. I was happy to be there and to be able to compete amongst the best swimmers in the world. I had spent years swimming four to six hours a day—and years away from the pool, when I just needed to take a break from the smell of chlorine and the rigorous training.

Wherever I was in my life, a few things remained constant: I was always driven by my goals. During my years of training, the thing that got me out of my warm, cozy bed at 5:30 a.m. was imagining the medals I wanted to win and envisioning myself standing up on the Olympic podium. When I retired from swimming, my goals shifted. I was more focused on being the best mom that I could be and being a successful businesswoman.

In addition to being goal-driven, the other constant for me was a determination to give every endeavor my all. Knowing that I tried my best in the pool or anywhere else has always been my measure of success. As an athlete, I'm sure you get that. Know that the hours you put into practice, your hard work, sacrifice, dedication, ability to stay focused on a goal, and your competitive spirit will serve you for the rest of your life.

And don't forget to have fun,

DARA TORRES
5-time Olympian

INTRODUCTION

When Megan Rapinoe was a little girl, she ran outside to kick a ball on a soccer field that looked a lot like the one behind your school. When Michelle Kwan put on her first ice skates, she wobbled out onto the ice just like any other rookie skater. And when Rebecca Lobo first grabbed a basketball from one of her siblings and bounce, bounce, bounced it on the blacktop, it could have been the blacktop at your local park.

The world's best athletes picked up their skills in neighborhood parks and on unremarkable streets. They were just like you: girls with big dreams, who loved to run or swim or bike or just to play for hours and hours with their friends. Eventually, they realized they were really, really good at soccer—or skating, or basketball, or tennis, or kayaking, or one of dozens more sports. But that was only one piece of the puzzle. All of the women in this book—gold medalist Olympians, national champions, world champions—realized that if they wanted to make their dreams come true in sports, they had to work hard, to spend hundreds of hours shooting hoops or swinging bats or swinging their golf clubs. They knew it might be grueling, that they might have to give up movie night with their friends or get their homework done quickly, but the sacrifices were worth it. They also knew that there were few opportunities to earn a living playing the sports they loved. Roster spots were harder to come by than they were for the boys in their classes. In some cases, there weren't even pro leagues or Olympic events in the sports these girl athletes played, like boxing, which didn't have women's Olympic events until 2012.

But that didn't stop them. It only made them stronger, and the reason women's sports leagues and organizations like the Ladies Professional Golf Association (LPGA), Women's National Basketball Association (WNBA), National Women's Soccer League (NWSL) and National Women's Hockey League (NWHL) exist is because of the girls and women in these pages who refused to hang up their uniforms. Sometimes they played with teams full of boys. Sometimes they were shamed for looking different, for the color of their skin, and they kept on training regardless. They quieted critics with backflips and backhands, 3-pointers and 360-degree spins on their skateboards.

Being a girl athlete isn't always easy. It's sweaty and frustrating. It can lead to injuries and heartbreak—but injuries heal with hard work, and there's always another race to run or game to play. These girl athletes have played in front of packed arenas and set world records. They've designed clothing lines and written books, had babies and run marathons and traveled from Paris to Pyeongchang to Peru. But not so long ago, they were girls just like you, playing on school teams and club teams or with their best friends from down the block. They had goals that sometimes seemed impossible, and they smashed them. You can too!

—JOAN NIESEN

Bethany Hamilton

THERE **IS NO** SUCH THING AS A HANDICAP

One bright, sunny morning in 2003, 13-year-old Bethany Hamilton went out to surf with a friend and her family at a beach near their homes in Hawaii. Bethany had been competing for five years at that point and was widely considered a rising star in the surfing world. While riding the waves that day in Kauai, Bethany was attacked by a 14-foot-long tiger shark, which quickly and cleanly severed her left arm below her shoulder. She clung to her surfboard so she would not get pulled under as the shark dragged her back and forth. Then she made it back to shore with the help of her surfing companions. Her friend's father used a surfboard leash (the cord that wraps around surfers' ankles, connecting them to their boards in case they wipe out) to try to slow the bleeding from Bethany's shoulder. The group sped to a hospital, and by the time they arrived, Bethany had lost more than 60% of the blood in her body. In shock, she was rushed into surgery. Amazingly, she survived.

Though returning to the site of a terrifying attack might not appeal to most people, a month after the incident, Bethany was back in the water and on her surfboard, determined not to let her injury separate her from the sport she loved. "If I don't get back on my board, I'll be in a bad mood forever," she told ABC News. She wasn't going to give up on her goal of becoming a professional surfer.

"Ultimately I'm driven by my passion and love for riding waves," Bethany told NPR in 2019. "You know, so many people are like, 'Why would you get back into the ocean with sharks?' and I'm like, 'Well, I just have more fear of losing this love that I have for riding waves.'"

At first, Bethany used a special surfboard to help her adjust to her new body, finding balance with just one arm. The adaptive board was custom-made, a bit longer and thicker than the one she'd previously used. It also had a handle for her right arm, making it easier to paddle. Her legs got stronger as she learned to kick harder to help make up for any power she'd lost. Not even three months after the attack, Bethany returned to competition, and in 2004, she also wrote an autobiography, *Soul Surfer: A True Story of Faith, Family, and Fighting to Get Back on the Board.* It became a bestseller, and then a movie.

It wasn't long before Bethany traded in her custom surfboard for a standard model. She didn't need that extra help anymore, even with just one arm. Within two years of the attack, Bethany competed in the championships run by the NSSA (National Scholastic Surfing Association) and won—riding the waves at Salt Creek Beach in Orange County better than she had with two arms. Two years later, at 17, Bethany turned pro, realizing her dream.

> "COURAGE, SACRIFICE, DETERMINATION, COMMITMENT, TOUGHNESS, HEART, TALENT, GUTS. THAT'S WHAT LITTLE GIRLS ARE MADE OF; **THE HECK WITH SUGAR AND SPICE.**"

In 2016, she was nominated for a prestigious ESPY, one of the annual awards ESPN gives to athletes for their accomplishments in and outside of sports. She'd won an ESPY before, in 2004, for Best Comeback Athlete, but this time, after more than a decade of surfing without her left arm, she was entered into a different category: Best Female Athlete with a Disability. Bethany pulled herself out of the running. She explained that she has huge respect for disabled athletes, but she doesn't view herself as belonging in that category.

Sixteen years to the day after the tiger shark attacked her, Bethany took a trip to the stretch of water off Tunnels Beach where she'd lost her left arm. On this anniversary, she posted on Facebook: "I can be here with contentedness knowing that from awful times beauty can come. . . . Cheers to life and all the craziness and beauty we face. We can choose who we become through it all!"

THE NEXT FEARLESS MOVE

Throughout her career, Bethany has always been looking for a new challenge, whether it was re-learning how to surf after her accident, getting back in shape after her kids' births, or even competing on *The Amazing Race* with her husband. (They finished third.) In recent years, she's spent tons of time working on aerial moves on her surfboard. Relatively new to surfing, an aerial requires riding the board up the wave and then into the air above its lip (the top edge). Competitors try to incorporate aerials as much as they can. The move demands great balance and coordination, as well as fearlessness. Before they can launch themselves over a wave, surfers need to gain good speed, crouch low, and then turn almost sideways in the air. Bethany traveled as far as Indonesia in 2014 to work on aerials, visiting Padang Padang beach, where she practiced over and over in the fast waves, eventually pulling off a front side air-reverse 360, in which she surfed up off the wave while rotating 360 degrees, a full turn, in the air.

Wilma Rudolph

JUST BECAUSE YOU CAN'T WALK **DOESN'T MEAN** YOU WON'T RUN

Wilma Rudolph was born prematurely on June 23, 1940, weighing just 4.5 pounds. And as she grew from baby to toddler to child, that small size at birth was the least of her (and her parents') worries. Before she turned five, Wilma had contracted scarlet fever, polio, and double pneumonia—three diseases that could easily have killed her. Polio left her partially paralyzed.

To help her walk, Wilma wore a brace on her weak left leg for years, and she needed plenty of attention from doctors to help her condition improve. But Wilma was Black, and in the 1940s, that meant she had limited access to health care in her home state of Tennessee. She and her mother were forced to ride a bus 100 miles round-trip each week to visit historically Black Meharry Medical College, in Nashville, for treatment. That routine lasted for years, and Wilma's family members (she had 21 siblings!) had to learn to help care for her at home, massaging her weak leg and foot several times a day. Nursing Wilma back to health was a huge group effort, but by the time Wilma was six, she could hop around on one foot. At 12, she was finally able to walk without leg braces or orthopedic shoes. "The doctor told me I would never walk again," Wilma wrote in her autobiography. "My mother told me I would. I believed my mother."

Because of Wilma's frequent illnesses, she wasn't able to attend kindergarten or first grade. When she did start elementary school, she was still physically limited, unable to play at full speed on the playground like the other kids. It wasn't until Wilma was in eighth grade that she began to consider playing sports. By then, her leg worked as well as anyone else's. She followed the example of her older sister, Yvonne, who was a gifted basketball player. Wilma took to the court, trying out for her high school team the next year. She was a natural, and as a high school sophomore, just two years after she started to play, she set a state record by scoring 803 points in the season.

Much of Wilma's basketball success came due to her speed on the court. Her coach, impressed by how fast she'd streak from basket to basket, gave her the nickname "Skeeter" because he thought she moved as quickly as a mosquito. During a state basketball championship match, Tennessee State's track and field coach, Ed Temple, also noticed Wilma's speed on the court. He invited her to train with him at the college over the summer. She was so talented that at 16, just four years after first walking unassisted, she qualified to participate in the 1956 Summer Olympics. In Australia, she won a bronze medal, running third in the 4x100-meter relay.

"RUNNING, AT THE TIME, WAS NOTHING BUT PURE ENJOYMENT FOR ME. I LOVED THE FEELING OF **FREEDOM** . . . THE FRESH AIR, THE FEELING THAT THE ONLY PERSON I'M REALLY COMPETING AGAINST IN THIS IS ME."

Wilma decided to extend her track career in college, racing at Tennessee State and training with Coach Temple. She was still a student when she competed in her second Olympics in 1960, this time in Rome. There, she won three gold medals: one in that same relay event and two in individual events, the 100-meter and 200-meter dashes. The relay was a special victory—all four women attended Tennessee State, and the college teammates set a world record in the preliminaries. During the finals, the temperature rose higher than 100 degrees, but the team managed to finish just one-tenth of a second off of their world record, securing the gold. "When I ran," Wilma said, "I felt like a butterfly that was free."

Those Olympics thrust Wilma into the spotlight, and she was celebrated in appearances throughout Europe. When she returned to the United States, her hometown wanted to host a homecoming parade, but Wilma said she would only attend if all people were welcome, regardless of their skin color. The parade became the first integrated public event ever held in Clarksville, Tennessee. After she graduated from college with a teaching degree, Wilma retired from racing in 1962 at just 22 years old, stating that she wanted to leave the game while she was still at her peak rather than decline in public. For the rest of her life, she taught, coached, and participated in civil rights causes.

Wilma passed away from throat cancer at age 54. In the world of track, she's remembered most for her graceful style of running, which was in part a product of her long-held joy at simply being able to do so.

Megan Rapinoe

BE PROUD, BE LOUD

When Megan Rapinoe was 14 years old, she watched the U.S. women's national team win the 1999 World Cup in a riveting penalty shoot-out in her home state of California. Megan, all of her friends, and her twin sister, Rachael, cheered as they watched the games and dreamed of getting the chance to represent their country on the field one day. Mia Hamm (see page 84), Julie Foudy, Brandi Chastain, Kristine Lilly and their teammates were Megan's idols. With that championship win, they put women's soccer in the spotlight. Now, two decades later, Megan considers those superstars to be her friends and mentors.

Megan was already on the path to the U.S. women's national team when the U.S. women won that unforgettable World Cup. As a talented teen soccer player, she skipped competing for her high school and instead suited up for the Elk Grove Pride, a local club team that was one of the best in the country. There, she developed a reputation for her crafty style of play and dexterity with the soccer ball. She says that including variety in her training helped her develop those skills. In fact, Megan competed in track and basketball for much of high school. Her strong play as a winger for Elk Grove earned her a spot (along with Rachael) on the University of Portland's roster. While Megan was in college, she began to compete with the national team, and she also helped lead Portland to a national championship. In 2006, just a few months after first playing with the national team,

> **"MY MOM'S LIKE, 'WHY DO YOU ALWAYS HAVE TO TAKE IT ALL ON?' AND I DON'T KNOW. IT JUST FEELS NORMAL AND NATURAL TO ME."**

Megan scored her first goal in a friendly game against the Chinese Taipei national team. In fact, she scored two goals that day, and she hasn't looked back.

Megan was the second pick in the 2009 Women's Professional Soccer (WPS) draft in 2009, going to the Chicago Red Stars. Two years later, she had her biggest moment yet on the national stage when she kicked a dazzling pass across the field to Abby Wambach in the 122nd minute of the World Cup quarterfinal game. Wambach immediately scored, tying the score, and the U.S. won in overtime. "I just took a touch and smacked it with my left foot," Megan said of the pass. "I don't think I've hit a ball like that with my left foot." The team placed second in that World Cup, and a year later, they won gold in the 2012 Olympics, thanks in large part to Megan's three goals and four assists.

That same year, Megan publicly came out as a lesbian. In an interview with *USA Today*, she said that the response had "been extremely positive, which makes me really happy." Since then, Megan has used her voice to highlight issues. "It is important for girls to be unapologetic for what they believe in and for what they want to get out of competing in sports," Megan said. "The power of the collective is something that they can gain strength from as they tackle the challenges and obstacles in life."

In 2015, Megan helped lead the U.S. women to their first World Cup title since she joined the team, and three years later, in advance of the 2019 World Cup, Megan was named a co-captain of the national team. That's when she proved she was something more than just a star soccer player. Tired of accepting lower pay than their male counterparts (while racking up a much better record on the field), the

U.S. women's team filed a lawsuit in 2019, suing for equal pay. Megan helped lead the effort. "We won't accept anything less than equal pay," she said on *Good Morning America*. "We show up for a game, if we win the game, if we lose the game, if we tie the game, we want to be paid equally, period."

By then, Megan was used to speaking up about injustices. She'd been doing it for years. In 2015, when NFL quarterback Colin Kaepernick began kneeling during the national anthem to protest oppression of minorities, Megan expressed support for his position. She has stood in silence or knelt during anthems, even as the U.S. Soccer Federation opposed that decision. Between that protest and the lawsuit, she's garnered criticism—which she's ignored in favor of following her heart and her beliefs. Publicly, she's spoken out against former President Donald Trump and his policies, and he's fired back at her. "We are everything he loves," Megan said of the president to *The Guardian*, "with the exception that we're powerful, strong women."

And in the 2019 World Cup, no one was more powerful or stronger than Megan and the U.S. team, whose play backed up the claims that they were worth more than they were earning. The women won the tournament handily, and Megan played a huge role in the win, celebrating every triumph with her signature move, thrusting her chest out and opening her arms wide at her sides, as if inviting the crowd to roar. Though she was battling an injured hamstring, she missed just one game and was able to suit up for the final against the Netherlands. There, she scored the 50th international goal of her career on a penalty kick. It was one of two goals in the game, both scored by the U.S., and when ball hit net, Megan became the oldest woman (at 34) to score in a World Cup Final. She was also awarded the Golden Boot, which goes to the tournament's top scorer, and the Golden Ball, given to the tournament's best player. At the ticker-tape parade thrown in New York City when the women returned, Megan got her moment with the trophy, kissing it and proclaiming, "I deserve this!"

Rebecca Lobo

STAND UP FOR YOUR SPORT

Standing 6'4" by the time she went to college, Rebecca Lobo seemed destined to be a basketball star. Both of her older siblings played, and she was always taller than nearly everyone her age. As a standout center on her high school team in Southwick, Massachusetts, Rebecca was recruited by more than 100 colleges to continue her basketball career at the next level. She chose the University of Connecticut (UConn) because of its strong academics and it was close to her hometown.

Back then, UConn women's basketball was an upstart, not the dynasty it is today. The season before Rebecca joined the team, it made a surprise run to the Final Four, which was big news for a team that had never made it so far in the NCAA Tournament. When Rebecca came aboard, the team hoped to make another run—but no one had any idea that the lanky freshman would kick off several decades of huge success for the Huskies. UConn was one of the 64 teams to make it to the NCAA tournament every year Rebecca was on the team, and as a senior in 1995, Rebecca was the best player in the game. She won multiple awards recognizing her as women's college basketball's top player, and she led UConn to an undefeated 35-0 record. The school won its first national championship at the end of that season.

Then Rebecca graduated. The WNBA hadn't been founded yet, so her options were limited. She joined the existing women's national

"THERE'S NOTHING MASCULINE ABOUT BEING COMPETITIVE. THERE'S NOTHING MASCULINE ABOUT TRYING TO BE THE BEST AT EVERYTHING YOU DO, NOR IS THERE ANYTHING WRONG WITH IT."

basketball team as its youngest player, and though she played fewer minutes than most of her teammates, she still helped propel the U.S. team to its gold medal win at the 1996 Olympics. A year later, when the WNBA launched, Rebecca was the second player assigned to a team. The New York Liberty were thrilled to have her, and they knew they were getting one of the most unique women to ever play the game. Rebecca was tall, a strong center who could muscle her way underneath the basket, but in moments, she could also play like a guard, sinking 3-point shots as well as anyone else. In her first season of professional hoops, Rebecca made it all the way to the WNBA Finals, where the Liberty lost to Houston.

Rebecca was selected to the league's first all-star game two years later, but she tore her ACL and wasn't able to compete. She missed the 2000 season as a result of the injury, and in 2001, back on the court and healthy, she happened to meet a *Sports Illustrated* writer in Manhattan. She recognized Steve Rushin as the person who had mocked the WNBA in a recent article for the magazine, claiming that people were "snoring in the stands." Rebecca asked him how many women's games he'd been to. The answer was zero. Rebecca informed the writer that the Liberty drew 15,000 fans to its games most days and invited him to see the excitement for himself. He accepted, and two years later, the pair were married.

Rebecca retired from basketball in 2003, and she was admitted into the Women's Basketball Hall of Fame in 2010. In her speech at the induction ceremony, she told a story about her daughter, who was four years old at the time. Rebecca explained that her husband had been watching a basketball game on television in the family's living room, and the little girl was confused. "My daughter walked in the room and looked at the TV and said to Steve, 'Are those boys playing?'," Rebecca said. She told her daughter that yes, there was a boys' game on TV, and her daughter replied: "I didn't know boys played basketball."

In addition to bringing more attention to the women's game—both in her household and across the United States—Rebecca drew in new fans of Latino heritage. When she accepted her scholarship at UConn, Rebecca, whose father is Cuban, was one of the few Latina players at the highest levels of the game, and by the time she made it to the WNBA, she was attracting fans from that community. "I remember being with the Houston Comets and playing a game in Los Angeles," Rebecca told ESPN. "There was a whole section in the Staples Center filled with Hispanic boys and girls who came to cheer me on. Pretty amazing."

In 2013, Rebecca joined ESPN as a commentator, and she concentrated on women's basketball and colorfully bringing it to life for a wider audience. In recent years, she's discussed a variety of topics, including refereeing and the seemingly inconsistent number of fouls called from season to season, which makes players uncertain how aggressive they're permitted to be. That kind of knowledge and analysis has made Rebecca a favorite on broadcasts. She was inducted into the Naismith Memorial Basketball Hall of Fame, which includes both men and women, in 2017.

6 FEET 4 INCHES

Simone Biles

PUSH THE LIMITS

In 2013, at just 16 years old, Simone Biles attempted a skill in her floor exercise routine that had never been perfected before at the highest levels of gymnastics. On her way to winning the world all-around title in her first major international meet, Simone executed a double layout with a half twist on the floor. That means that with her body in a straight position, she did two backflips, turning 180-degrees during the second flip. If a gymnast is the first person to perfectly execute a new move in either the World Championships, like Simone did, or the Olympics, then that move is officially named after that gymnast in the code of points of the international gymnastics governing body. So on that fall day in Belgium, Simone, and The Biles, made history.

It would take another five years for Simone to add more skills to the code of points. At the 2018 World Championships, Simone performed a feat on the vault that had never been done, and another Biles entered the official gymnastics points code. A year later, Simone added two more: a double-twisting double-tucked somersault dismount on the balance beam and a "triple-double" element in her floor routine. In the "triple-double," Simone rotated on an imaginary axis through her hips twice *while at the same time* rotating around another imaginary axis from head to toe three times. She looked like a human top arcing through the air, and when she landed it, she had pulled off the most difficult feat of her career—and in all of women's gymnastics. The Biles II, as the floor exercise element is called, earned a rating of "J" in the code of points. Before Simone completed it, the hardest element in the code had a degree of difficulty of "I." The sport invented a new category for Simone.

The Biles

Then in May of 2021, Simone landed a Yurchenko Double Pike off a vault—something no other woman had even attempted in competition. The move is so challenging that the gymnastics judges seemed to decide they would not reward it—either because they did not want to encourage other gymnasts to attempt such a dangerous move, or because they felt that nobody could possibly compete with Simone if the difficulty of her moves was weighted appropriately. She was definitively in a league of her own.

Though she often makes gymnastics look easy, Simone overcame many obstacles before her first dismount. When she was three years old, Simone and her siblings were put in foster care because their mother, who struggled with substance abuse, was unable to take care of them. When she was six, Simone moved to Houston to live with her grandparents who adopted her and her younger sister. It was there that Simone was invited to work out at a local gymnastics center and began to display surprising upper-body strength, climbing a rope nearly all the way to the ceiling without really trying. That super-human strength propelled her body in gravity-defying ways.

Standing just 4'8", Simone is a tiny package of nearly all muscle. As a child, she was often shamed for her muscular arms and for a long time, she struggled with body image issues. "I've learned to put on a strong front and let most of it slide," she said in a social media post. "But I'd be lying if I told you that what people say about my arms, my legs, my body . . . of how I look in a dress, leotard, bathing suit or even in casual pants hasn't gotten me down at times." But she learned to embrace her body and has spoken out to other young gymnasts about celebrating the physical strength that comes with those muscles.

Her mental strength has played a sizable role in her success as well. She's able to focus, to spend hours and hours in the gym, and somehow manages to make it look effortless. The truth is that Simone was diagnosed with attention-deficit/hyperactivity disorder (ADHD) as a young girl. She has taken medication to treat it for years, though she says that even before being medicated, she was able to be "laser-focused" on gymnastics. "At school, teachers had started talking to my parents about my lack of concentration in the classroom," Simone wrote in her autobiography. "It seemed that any little thing—a bird flitting by outside, footsteps in the hallway, one student whispering to another at the back of the room—was enough to distract me from what the teacher was saying."

> **"THE SAME THING THAT'S TRUE IN GYMNASTICS IS ALSO TRUE IN LIFE: YOU CAN'T GO BACK. THE BEST YOU CAN DO IS FORGIVE YOURSELF, TAKE A DEEP BREATH, AND GET TO WORK ON THE NEXT CHALLENGE."**

Simone has been vocal in recent years about her ADHD and the fact that it's OK to ask for help. More than 11% of children are diagnosed with ADHD at some point in their lives, so her message was important to many of her fans, helping them to realize that even their favorite athletes have battles of their own.

Simone's bravery—in pushing herself physically, and by opening up about her personal challenges—has inspired a generation of girls who struggle, and strive, as well.

Kara Goucher

KEEP THE **FUN** IN THE RUN

From the time she was six years old, trailing her grandfather in a local one-mile fun run, Kara Goucher has loved running. Kara's "Papa" was a runner who encouraged his three granddaughters to be athletic. By third grade, she'd discovered that she was fast—which was a good thing, because she didn't like to lose. In high school in Duluth, Minnesota, Kara was swift enough to help her team win multiple state cross-country titles. Her coach taught her that "running for pure pleasure is the surest way to run well," a lesson that has served her well over her decades-long career.

At the University of Colorado, the stakes were much higher, and Kara learned the critical art of pacing from her coach, Mark Wetmore. He encouraged her to let other people go out harder at the start of races so that she could save her fuel for later on. That training secret made racing far less painful, and it transformed her into a breakout star. Kara was the NCAA Outdoor Champion in the 3,000- and 5,000-meter races and looked poised to have a successful career as a runner when she finished college in 2001.

But that's not what happened. Instead, injuries began to nag Kara. It took a full five years, until 2006, before she was healthy and back in top form. That year, Kara finished second in the 5K at the USA Track and Field (USATF) Outdoor Championships and then began competing internationally, setting personal records in nearly every race she won. At the World Cup race in 2006, Kara's 10K time made her the second-fastest American woman to run that distance. "It was an affirmation for me that I was doing the right thing with my life," Kara told LetsRun.com after her big year.

To help their careers, Kara and her husband (who was also an Olympic runner) had moved to Oregon to train. Her new routine involved running more than she ever had in her life—averaging 85 miles per week during her most intense training periods. Kara spent time strength training and running on an anti-gravity treadmill to help reduce injury risk, and she trained at higher altitude to improve her lung capacity.

For the next few years, Kara was at the top of her game and earned a lucrative Nike sponsorship. She ran the fastest half marathon time of any woman in 2007 in her first-ever half marathon, and she competed in the 2008 Olympics in Beijing. She also ran her first marathon that year, placing third in New York.

In September, 2010, at the age of 32, Kara gave birth to a baby boy named Colton—but what should have been a joyful time for her was instead stressful. Shortly after she became pregnant, Kara learned that Nike wouldn't pay her if she wasn't racing—and training and competing during her pregnancy would have been dangerous. Still, she planned to run a half marathon three months after giving birth, and she rushed back into training a week after Colton was born. Colton became ill and had to go to the hospital. As a new mom, Kara had to choose between getting a paycheck (which required training and racing), or being with her son. She chose running, and her commitment paid off with a personal best time at the 2011 Boston Marathon, six months after giving birth. But Kara regretted her choice. She told the *New York Times*, "Looking back and knowing that I wasn't the kind of mother I want to be—it's gut-wrenching." Lots of things were starting to feel wrong. Kara was worried about her age and about a recurring foot injury. At the 2012 Outdoor Championships, she was so disappointed in her finish, she burst into tears as she left the track.

Running had become stressful. It was time for a change. In 2014, Kara and her husband sold their house and moved back to Colorado, where they met during college. Kara reunited with Wetmore, her former coach, and found new sponsors. Her injured foot began to feel better thanks to physical therapy. Things didn't go perfectly—Kara had to deal with a back injury while training for the Boston Marathon—but she was starting to feel in control of her life again. She pushed herself while training with younger teammates in spite of worrying that she couldn't keep up. "They've forced me to believe in myself and to see, 'Oh, that wasn't so scary,'" Kara told Flotrack.org.

Rejuvenated, Kara won the Rock 'n' Roll Half Marathon in San Antonio in 2014 and came in fourth in the marathon at the Olympic Trials in 2016. She hasn't represented the United States since then, but even as she's entered her 40s and aged out of Olympic contention, she's still exploring new challenges in the world of running. She took up trail running, which happens on unpaved (grass, dirt, or rocks), often steep trails. It can be intimidating for anyone—and terrifying for someone who's suffered as many injuries as Kara had over the course of her career. But facing her fear and trying something new was the point.

Kara finished fifth overall and first in her age group in her first trail-running marathon in 2019. She described it as the hardest thing she'd ever accomplished— which somehow made her want to run even further the next time out. Months later, Kara placed third in a 50K ultramarathon. She found success—and joy—winding around the trees.

"I'D RATHER BE DINGED UP KARA WITH THE BAD KNEE WHO'S A LITTLE BIT OLDER BUT WHO'S STILL GETTING OUT THERE THAN BE KARA WHO'S TOO AFRAID TO TRY."

Mikaela Shiffrin

FOCUS ON **YOUR SPORT,** NOT YOUR STATS

Mikaela Shiffrin grew up on the ski slopes. Born in the mountain town of Colorado, she spent most of her childhood there and in rural New Hampshire, where she was able to take advantage of the northeast United States' best ski territory and even attend a skiing-focused school. The sport came naturally to her, in part because it was almost always available in her backyard, and by the time she turned 15 and was qualified to compete in World Cup events, Mikaela was prepared to take on the world's best skiers.

In 2011, at 16, Mikaela made her first podium in a World Cup race in dramatic fashion, losing her shin guard on her first run before zipping expertly through her second and winning third place. That race was the start of an impressive career that's put Mikaela into the conversation as one of the greatest skiers of all time. She told *The Denver Post*, "When I ski, it's like a song. I can hear the rhythm in my head, and when I start to ski that rhythm and I start to really link my turns together, all of a sudden there's so much flow and power that I just can't help but feel amazing. That's where the joy comes from."

Mikaela nabbed her first Olympic gold medal in 2014 in Sochi, weeks before she turned 19. Four years later in Pyeongchang for the 2018 Olympics, she was at it again, an easy bet to win most of her events. She took another gold in giant slalom and a silver in the combined event, in which skiers compete in one downhill run and

"SKIING IS MY ART."

two slaloms and are graded on their total time.

The year 2018 turned out to be a history-making one for Mikaela. When she won a super-G race at the World Cup in Lake Louise, Canada, skiing downhill, through gate after gate and making turn after turn at speeds even faster than a traditional downhill competition, she became the first athlete ever to win an event in each of the six different categories in which a skier can compete. She'd already won World Cup races in the other events: slalom, parallel slalom, giant slalom, downhill and alpine, and adding the super-G to her list of accomplishments sealed her record.

A year later at the World Championships in Sweden, Mikaela began to feel like she couldn't master six events at once. She'd been successful at all of them before, but she had a hunch that it wasn't smart to try to master so many events at the same competition. She knew that pushing herself too far could have negative consequences. The previous year in Pyeongchang, she had struggled in the slalom, feeling overwhelmed by schedule changes due to weather. She was out of sorts, threw up before the race, and placed fourth. She did not want to repeat the experience. What's more, she was fighting a lung

SKI RACING 101

The best skiers in the world are often some of the most versatile, able to compete in all or most of the different events sanctioned by the International Ski Federation: slalom, parallel slalom, giant slalom, super-G, downhill, and alpine combined. Mikaela has medaled in all of them, but there are huge differences between every event.

In **slalom** events, precision is key. Skiers must move through a winding course, avoiding obstacles. In **parallel slalom**, two skiers compete head-to-head on identical slalom courses. In **giant slalom**, the obstacles are placed farther apart than in slalom, and in **super-G**, they're placed even farther apart. In **downhill**, speed is the most important component, and skiers are challenged to move straight ahead down the hill as quickly as they can. And finally, the **alpine combined event** involves multiple races. Skiers complete one downhill run and two slalom runs on separate days, and their scores are totaled to see who comes in with the lowest combined time.

infection. So, after winning gold in the super-G race, Mikaela decided to skip the combined event in Sweden, instead resting and concentrating on other races she wanted to win later in the championships. When she announced she wouldn't be skiing in the combined, Bode Miller and Lindsey Vonn (see page 110), two of the greatest skiers of their generation, both said they'd have raced if they were in Mikaela's shoes as an overwhelming favorite. The break was worth it, though. Mikaela won a bronze in the giant slalom and a gold in the slalom.

"From the outside, people see the records and stats," Mikaela wrote after the championships. "As I have said, those numbers dehumanize the sport and what every athlete is trying to achieve. What I see is an enormous mixture of work, training, joy, heartache, motivation, laughs, stress, sleepless nights, triumph, pain, doubt, certainty, more doubt, more work, more training, surprises, delayed flights, canceled flights, lost luggage, long drives through the night, expense, more work, adventure, and some races mixed in there."

Mikaela wants to ski well every time she starts a race, not to feel over-extended or anxious at the number of races on her schedule. And she wants her career to continue for as long as possible. She does not want to get sidelined by burnout or injuries. She posted on Instagram, "It is clear to me that many believe I am approaching my career in a way that nobody has before, and people don't really understand it. But you know what?! That is completely fine by me, because I am ME, and no one else." In the 2021 World Championships in Italy, she earned another 4 medals.

By being herself, Mikaela is setting records without making that her focus. By the time she retires (years from now, she hopes), she'll be remembered as one of the best in the history of skiing, despite doing things on her own terms, or maybe because of it.

Althea Gibson

DON'T BE AFRAID TO BE
THE FIRST

Althea Gibson was born in a sharecropper's shack in South
Carolina in the summer of 1927, but her family moved to New
York City during the Great Depression when she was just a baby. In
her new home, far from fields and open spaces, she spent much of
her time in the street. Near the family's Harlem apartment, a portion
of 143rd Street was barricaded from cars, and children used the
traffic-free space to play sports. An amazing piece of luck placed a
paddle tennis court just steps from Althea's door, and that's where
she learned to play. (Paddle tennis is a variation on traditional tennis,
where players use what looks like a large Ping-Pong paddle. The court
is smaller than a tennis court and doesn't have doubles lanes.)

In the 1930s, tennis was not a sport that welcomed African
American men or women. Tournaments were held at white-only
clubs, and there weren't accessible public courts. Still, Althea was
a natural—good enough to turn heads, especially when she won
the New York City women's paddle tennis championship at age
12. Members of a Black tennis club in Harlem offered her a junior
membership, but Althea wasn't in love with the sport yet. She
wanted to play games that she thought were tougher than tennis.

When she dropped out of school at 13, she had more time
to devote to hobbies she loved, like watching movies and playing
basketball. Around that time, she also took up street fighting, helping

to protect her family and herself in a neighborhood where violence could break out at any moment. In her autobiography, *I Always Wanted to Be Somebody*, Althea wrote that back then, she was "living pretty wild."

Eventually, Althea began to play tennis competitively, but she did it her own way. Her hair was cut short, and she wore shorts instead of skirts. She was strong, scrappy, and effective, and people, including two African American doctors who were hoping to help integrate tennis, began to notice her talent. The doctors took interest in Althea's career, providing her with more advanced coaching and happily watching her improve. Althea was tall and thin, with a wide wingspan. "My style of play, I believe, was aggressive, dynamic, and mean," she said in an educational film after she retired.

Although she was clearly an accomplished player, Althea's applications to tournaments were initially rejected due to her skin color. Eventually, though, tennis organizers at the highest levels relented, and she was invited to play in the U.S. national championships (now the U.S. Open). Althea was the first African American to play there and at Wimbledon, where she debuted in 1951. These two tournaments along with the French Open and Australian Open comprise the Grand Slam, the most prestigious tournaments in tennis. Althea was a gifted player, and her game really

IT'S LONELY AT THE TOP

In her later years, Althea felt alone once again. As her health declined, few tennis fans realized she'd suffered from brain disease and a stroke. She did tell her dear friend and former doubles partner, Angela Buxton, who reached out to the tennis world for support. Money poured in to help Althea turn her life around. Young tennis players, in a sport that had become more diverse since the 1950s, revered her. Venus Williams talked about Althea in the book *Women in Black History*. "I am honored to have followed in such great footsteps. Her accomplishments set the stage for my success, and through players like myself and Serena (see page 56) and many others to come, her legacy will live on."

took off when she started working with the coach Sydney Llewellyn. The two practiced together five days a week for eight hours each day. Sometimes Althea would serve 300 balls in a row before moving on. Another Black tennis player, Billy Davis, would join to compete against Althea. "We would play as if we were playing a match for our lives," she said. Althea worked her way up through the ranks of women's professional tennis until she won her first Grand Slam title at Wimbledon in 1957, which would become the year of Althea Gibson. She was the tournament's first Black champion, and she earned her victory decisively, winning in less than an hour. The *New York Times* wrote that Althea's serves were so powerful, her opponent could only lob them back. "Shaking hands with the Queen of England was a long way from being forced to sit in the colored section of the bus going into downtown Wilmington, North Carolina," Althea wrote about the win in her autobiography. New York celebrated her with a ticker-tape parade when she returned from overseas. Over her short career, Althea won 11 Grand Slam tournaments: five singles titles, five doubles titles and one mixed doubles title, all between 1956 and 1958.

Despite her success, and the public celebrations, Althea felt isolated in a game that was still primarily white. She retired in 1958, saying in her speech: "I hope that I have accomplished just one thing, that I have been a credit to tennis, and to my country."

"I WOULD HAVE ABOUT TWO OR THREE HUNDRED BALLS ON THE SERVICE LINE, AND I WOULD SERVE ALL OF THOSE BALLS IN ONE SPOT, UNTIL I WAS SO ACCURATE THAT I COULD CLOSE MY EYES AND PUT THE BALL WHERE I WANTED TO."

Janet Guthrie

USE YOUR **BRAINPOWER**

The daughter of two pilots, Janet Guthrie was born into a family that was focused on the sky in an era where America had set its sights on the stars. Janet grew up in Miami, Florida as the first moments of the space race unfolded. By the age of 16, she knew how to fly a plane, thanks to her father's instruction, and she'd also executed a parachute jump from the air. She knew exactly what she wanted to be when she grew up: an astronaut.

At the University of Michigan, Janet started out studying aeronautical engineering before switching her major to physics. After graduation, she moved to Long Island (a suburban area outside New York City) and worked in the aerospace industry, eventually applying to be an astronaut. Though she wasn't accepted into the program, Janet knew there were other ways she could apply her physics background to something more exciting and active than solving equations or performing experiments in a lab.

Janet had thought about buying a share of an airplane, but the New York airspace was too crowded to accommodate private pilots. So she settled on a car instead, purchasing a sleek Jaguar coupe. She drove her new ride to work—and then started using it to compete in races. "Oh, the Jaguar!" Janet once wrote in a story for *Physics World* magazine. "So beautiful, so prone to breakdowns! My heart still goes pit-a-pat whenever I see one of them."

Janet fell in love with racing, but unlike the men she competed against, she had no sponsorship money, so she had to be creative. She bought a station wagon for $45 and used it to tow her race car from event to event. The wagon also served as a makeshift hotel room. Janet wasn't earning money with her car-racing hobby, so she kept working as an engineer. Her engineering skills helped as she applied her scientific brilliance to building her own engine over the course of many years. But her obsession with engines and racing also conflicted with her career. She couldn't finish her master's degree in physics because racing season conflicted with final exams.

> **"THE CHARACTERISTICS THAT MAKE A GOOD RACING DRIVER ARE CONCENTRATION, DESIRE, JUDGMENT, AND EMOTIONAL DETACHMENT.** YOU CAN'T GET ANGRY BEHIND THE WHEEL.**"**

Janet's sacrifices paid off in 1976, when a racing team owner called her. Rolla Vollstedt wanted to get a woman into the all-male Indy 500 (a 500-mile race where drivers complete 200 laps of the course before crossing the finish line), and he wanted it to be Janet. His connections got her into big races that would help her qualify for the Indy 500, but Janet still lacked the financial resources of other male drivers with sponsors. She didn't have the cash to buy a new engine, which could cost as much as $10,000 back then, and instead she scrounged for used parts. When a sponsor, Coca-Cola, showed interest in 1976, Janet was thrilled—until she learned the company would pay her only if she wore all pink, the color of a can of Tab, their diet cola at the time. "At Indianapolis, a pink driver's suit would be like waving a red flag in a ring full of bulls," Janet wrote in her autobiography.

The next year, in 1977, Janet earned a spot in the Indy 500 and posted an average speed of 188.4 miles per hour in the qualifying race. It was a momentous occasion, marked by a small tweak to the event's traditional opening script: "In company with the first lady ever to qualify at Indianapolis," announcer and Speedway owner Tony Hulman said to kick off the race, "gentlemen, start your engines!"

Though many of the men competing didn't like to see her pull up beside them at the starting lines of races, Janet pulled up nonetheless and often passed them on the course. In her first Indy 500, she had equipment issues and placed 29th out of 33 racers. The next year, in 1978, despite breaking her wrist two days before the race, she came in ninth place. As Janet continued to compete, she began to realize how important the mental aspect of driving was, not only when she was tapping into her scientific knowledge to build and repair engines, but also right before a race, when she was able to find a state of calm amid the noise and speed of the track.

Because it remained so hard to get sponsorships, Janet retired from racing in 1980, just four years after she debuted. Her best finish was fifth place, but even without a first-place victory, she made history. Her face appears on racing trading cards, and her suit and helmet are part of the collection at the National Museum of American History. After retiring, Janet returned to her engineering career, but she never gave up her interest in cars. In 2011, she joined women's rights activists in petitioning to allow Saudi Arabian women to drive. (Women there finally earned that right in 2018.)

"I think it's just in some people's nature to want to find out what it's like out there at the edge of human capabilities," Janet explained to *Physics World*, when asked about her love of adventure, "and fortunately I was born in the machine age when broad shoulders and big muscles didn't make that much difference—didn't make any difference, in fact."

Mo'ne Davis

THROW LIKE A GIRL

Before Mo'ne Davis suited up to play in the 2014 Little League World Series, 17 other girls had played on the Little League's biggest stage. They'd won and lost, but no one had captured the public's attention quite like Mo'ne did. The show she put on started with a shutout on August 10, 2014, when she was pitching for Philadelphia's Taney Dragons, which hoped to be the mid-Atlantic region's representative in the World Series. That day, Mo'ne didn't allow a run, and her team won, 8-0. It came as no surprise when Mo'ne was picked to start Philadelphia's first World Series game, too.

That day, five days after her last shutout, Mo'ne did it again. The Dragons beat a team from Nashville, 4-0, advancing further into the tournament. Mo'ne made history with the win, becoming the first girl to win a Little League World Series game *and* the first to pitch a shutout there. (She was one of two girls in the tournament that year.) Suddenly, the whole world was watching her windup.

For those who'd known Mo'ne, her success was not surprising. When Mo'ne was seven, a coach who saw her play football with her cousins and brother was so impressed by the way she threw the ball in perfect spirals that he invited her to try basketball. Even though she'd barely hooped before, Mo'ne fit right in with the boys' team, and she was one of the best on the court. By the time Mo'ne was 10, she played point guard in basketball, pitched, fielded at shortstop and third base in baseball, and was a midfielder on her soccer team.

No matter how fast she was chasing a soccer ball or how high she could jump, Mo'ne was always known for her arm. That's how she kept playing baseball, kept starting games, and wound up at the Little League World Series at age 13 as her team's No. 1 starter. By then, Mo'ne had learned to throw a 70 mph fastball, which is at the high end for boys and girls in her age group. "Throwing 70 miles an hour, that's throwing like a girl," Mo'ne said after her World Series shutout.

She won the game with an inning that looked straight out of the movies. In the bottom of the sixth—the game's final inning—Mo'ne had a solid lead, but she wanted to keep her opponents off the scoreboard. She struck out the first batter, then the second. The third batter worked the count all the way to three balls and two strikes. Mo'ne had to make a solid pitch to avoid a walk, which she did, throwing a fastball right past him and over the plate. *Strike three, he's out!* Game over. Mo'ne had given up just two hits that day, with eight strikeouts to go along with them. The lucky charm in her back pocket—just a tiny bit of money in case she wanted to buy something to eat—had worked its magic.

"If I do stay into baseball, hopefully I can pitch, be a professional pitcher," she said after the victory.

Mo'ne's team won one more round before losing to a team from Nevada, which went on to win the United States bracket of the tournament. Despite the loss, Mo'ne was still the player everyone remembered long after the final out. Little girls around the world began to think they, too, could play baseball like Mo'ne.

"FIND A SPORT AND A CORE GROUP OF FRIENDS, WORK HARD, AND HAVE FUN WITH IT. THESE DAYS, A LOT OF PEOPLE CAN TAKE THE FUN AWAY."

Kate Courtney

FIND INSPIRATION IN **YOUR BACKYARD**

As a little girl growing up outside San Francisco, Kate Courtney lived in the shadow of Mount Tamalpais, the highest peak in the Marin Hills of California. It is a beautiful sight and also a giant playground for people who live in the vicinity. The peak is known for being the birthplace of mountain biking, and as a kid, Kate spent hours cycling on it, often on a tandem bicycle with her father, Tom.

As a teenager, Kate focused more on running, becoming devoted to her school's cross-country team. As a high school freshman, Kate decided to vary her workouts, and she added mountain biking back into the mix, this time on a traditional bicycle. At 14, she competed in a mountain bike race—which she won easily. That day, Kate left running behind, realizing that the joy she'd found on those childhood rides with her dad could actually become a career in sports.

It wasn't always easy. At a race in the Czech Republic during her junior year of high school, Kate was overwhelmed by European-style racing. She hadn't faced such skilled, aggressive riders before. "I finished tenth in that first race and was hooked," Kate told *Marin Magazine*. "The experience gave me so many things to work on, and I had done well enough that I had a glimmer of hope for improvement and success."

Kate began to race full-time after she graduated from Stanford

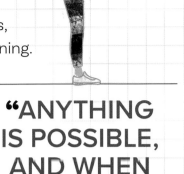

University in 2017. Competing in the under-23 age bracket, she won race after race, eventually landing a silver medal at her first U23 World Championship. Her success, she's said many times, comes from mental engagement and physical training. She works with a sports psychologist to get into the right headspace, and she also does yoga to unplug. "I try to focus on my own personal performance and the things that I can control," Kate said to *Marin Magazine*. "This mentality helps me look at races with optimism and excitement, thinking about how far I might be able to push myself and what I might be able to accomplish."

"ANYTHING IS POSSIBLE, AND WHEN YOU BELIEVE IN YOURSELF YOU CAN BE THE BEST."

In 2018, Kate flew to Lenzerheide, Switzerland, a mountain town in the middle of the Alps. There, she competed in the elite cross country race at the UCI Mountain Bike World Championships. She won a gold medal, the first American to do so since 2001. She was also awarded the rainbow jersey which is given to the world-champion cyclists every year. It's a distinct, recognizable jersey: white, with multicolored stripes across the torso. When Kate wore it across Europe, biking and visiting sites, strangers greeted and congratulated her in foreign languages. After a whirlwind trip, she returned home to California. On her first ride back in the U.S., she and her dad suited up for Mount Tamalpais, and when she put on the jersey, they both began to cry tears of joy.

Winners of the rainbow jersey only get to keep it for a year, so in 2019, on one of her last rides wearing it—no longer crisply white, but showing hints of dirt and sweat—Kate took her dad up Mount Tamalpais again. Though she gave up the jersey, she kept competing and in September 2019 became the first American mountain biker to lock down a spot for the Tokyo Olympics.

Babe Didrikson Zaharias

REINVENT YOURSELF

When Mildred Ella Didrikson was born in Port Arthur, Texas, in 1911, becoming a professional athlete was by no means a popular or even possible path for most girls. But with her almost superhuman gifts, she seemed destined to become a sports star from an early age. Mildred's power-hitting abilities in baseball earned her the nickname "Babe" (for Babe Ruth) as a child, and it stuck for most of her life. The daughter of Norwegian immigrants, Babe was extraordinarily gifted at every sport or task she tried. "All of my life I have always had the urge to do things better than anybody else," she said—and she did just that again and again.

After high school, Babe achieved her first big-time athletic success on the basketball court, leading her amateur team, the Dallas-based Golden Cyclones, to a championship in 1931. More than 60 years before the Women's National Basketball Association (WNBA) formed, Babe made headlines on the court, but there was no way for her to make a career out of playing hoops.

Shortly after that basketball championship, Babe decided to compete in the 1932 Amateur Athletic Association national track and field competition—as a team of one. Instead of joining a group to compete, like all the other women had, Babe felt she had the ability to rack up plenty of points on her own. She competed in eight events, often rushing from the finish line of one to the start of another. She excelled in everything from the discus throw to hurdles, winning five events. The 30 total points she earned at the meet were more than every other team.

At the Olympics that year in Los Angeles, Babe became truly world-famous. She won two gold medals (in the hurdles and javelin throw) and a silver in the high jump. (Back then, women were only allowed to compete in three track and field events. It's easy to imagine that Babe would have won even more gold medals if she'd been able to participate in more events!) "She is beyond all belief until you see her perform," Grantland Rice, a famous journalist, wrote of Babe. "Then you finally understand that you are looking at the most flawless section of muscle harmony, of complete mental and physical coordination, the world of sport has ever seen."

After taking the world of track and field by storm, Babe spent a few years experimenting in other sports. She played pool competitively and even pitched several innings of baseball in spring training in 1934, debuting with a no-hit inning before throwing for two more teams later that spring.

Although it looked as if she didn't have to try very hard to succeed, Babe's focus and intense dedication took her natural gifts to the next level. Babe was known for the hours she dedicated to every sport she played, putting up hundreds of basketball shots, high-jumping over and over, and perfecting her pitching with thousands of throws. "The formula for success is simple: practice and

TURNING WOMEN'S GOLF INTO A BUSINESS

Babe turned pro in golf in 1947, and when she did, she was just the eighth woman to ever become a professional on the links. She was making history, and her agent, Fred Corcoran, thought his client had a chance to do more than just win tournaments. Using Babe's talent and celebrity as leverage, Corcoran founded the Ladies Professional Golf Association (LPGA), which endures and thrives to this day. But at the start, the LPGA was mostly a vehicle to showcase Babe, and it relied largely on her corporate sponsors for funding. The tour got a $15,000 pledge in 1950 from a sports clothing company that allowed it to really take off, and once it did, Babe was the attraction that kept fans coming.

concentration, then more practice and more concentration," Babe once said.

By 1935, when she was just 24, Babe decided to move on to her third serious sport, a new challenge to which she dedicated herself: golf. In order to ease into the game, she hoped to compete against other non-professional athletes, but because of her fame and the money she'd already earned, she was not allowed to compete as an amateur. Before she even had a chance to really learn the game, Babe began competing against pro golfers. And just three years after learning to play golf, she became the first woman to compete against men in a Professional Golfer's Association (PGA) event in Los Angeles. Though she struggled there, she refused to give up, and by the early 1940s, she was the most dominant woman in the game. From 1940 to 1954, she won 10 LPGA major championships, and she continued to occasionally tee off against men, earning more and more success. In 1950, she had her best year ever on the links, winning all three women's major tournaments.

She continued to compete for much of the next five years despite battling cancer. Even as she underwent surgeries and treatments, some of which made her life uncomfortable and weakened her physically, she kept winning tournaments. Cancer was the single foe she could not defeat. She passed away in 1956, a year after winning her last tournament, when she was still the highest-ranked woman golfer in the world. All these years later, she still ranks as one of the best athletes of the last century and in 2021, she was posthumously awarded the Presidential Medal of Freedom in recognition of her achievements.

"THE BABE IS HERE. WHO'S COMING IN **SECOND?**"

Serena Williams

EMBRACE **YOUR** BODY AND STYLE

When Serena Williams was nine years old, she and her family moved from the Los Angeles area across the country to West Palm Beach, Florida. Serena and her older sister, Venus, were promising tennis players already, homeschooled by their father and in an intense training routine. But it was time for a change, and the family moved so the girls could attend an elite tennis academy.

While Serena and Venus were training there, their father still kept some control over their tennis careers, and he pulled them out of national junior tennis tournaments the year after the move. He wanted the girls to focus on school and take their careers slowly, and he also worried about the racism he already saw his daughters, who are African American, facing in a largely white sport. They looked different, and it made some people in the tennis world uncomfortable.

In 1995, at the age of 14, Serena went pro, and two years later, she began to climb the World Tennis Association rankings. In one tournament in 1997, she defeated the world's No. 7 and No. 4 players. Serena had arrived, and fans began to notice her powerful swing, which defined her game. In 1999, she won her first Grand Slam tournament at the U.S. Open, and she was unstoppable after that, winning in doubles at the U.S. Open and then contending at most Grand Slam events for the next decade. Starting with the French Open in 2002, Serena won four Grand Slam singles titles in a row and also won in doubles at Wimbledon and the Australian Open during that time. As she kept winning, her serve got stronger and stronger, topping out at 126.8 miles per hour in 2013. Only two women—one of whom is Venus—have ever served more powerfully, and opponents quickly learned to be terrified of that first whack, which would whiz by, expertly placed and impossible to hit. Serena has referred to her arm as "my weapon and machine," and she's also known for a backhand shot that's as devastating as her forehand, along with a signature open stance.

Over the course of her career, Serena has won 22 Grand Slam singles titles and another 12 Grand Slam doubles titles, but even at the top of the game—she's been ranked the No. 1 player in the world eight times—Serena still stands out for her body type, which is far more muscular than that of many of her opponents. She's even felt different from her sister Venus, whose build is long and lean. When Serena was younger, she found herself making unfair comparisons to Venus until her half-sister, Yetunde, helped her understand that beauty takes many forms. "What others marked as flaws or disadvantages about myself—my race, my gender—I embraced as fuel for my success," Serena wrote in an open letter to women in 2016. "I never let anything or anyone define me or my potential."

As early as 2002, Serena's fashion statements became as powerful as her strokes. At that year's U.S. Open—which Serena won, after winning at Wimbledon and the French Open earlier that season—she appeared in a black catsuit. Two years later,

> **"MY DREAM WASN'T LIKE THAT OF AN AVERAGE KID, MY DREAM WAS TO BE THE BEST TENNIS PLAYER IN THE WORLD. NOT THE BEST 'FEMALE' TENNIS PLAYER IN THE WORLD."**

she showed up to the U.S. Open wearing a denim skirt and knee-high boots. (Officials wouldn't let her play until she changed her footwear.) While warming up at Wimbledon in 2008, Serena sported a white trench coat made of a breathable and movable material that made it comfortable to play in, along with a bandanna and big hoop earrings.

In 2017, the action in Serena's life shifted off the court when she gave birth to her first child, a daughter named Olympia. Serena had life-threatening complications during childbirth and suffered from depression afterward. In fact, she was unable to get out of bed for six weeks after Olympia was born, and she had to postpone her return to the court. When she emerged, she was vocal about the difficulties that athletes who are mothers can face, while making a postpartum return to form look easy. In 2018, her first season back after childbirth, she lost in the finals at both Wimbledon and the U.S. Open. At the French Open, she broke out a catsuit, similar to the 2002 version. "Catsuit anyone?" she posted on Twitter. "For all the moms out there who had a tough recovery from pregnancy—here you go. If I can do it, so can you." In addition to the fact that she felt like a "warrior princess" in it, the catsuit served a medical purpose for Serena. The tight, stretchy fabric helped with circulation, preventing blood clots which had been a problem for her.

As much as Serena and many others liked the outfit, though, the French Tennis Federation did not, and it banned catsuits after the tournament. Nike, one of Serena's sponsors, responded to the ruling with an announcement of their own: "You can take the superhero out of her costume, but you can never take away her superpowers." And Serena got the last laugh of all. In 2019, she made it to the U.S. Open finals again. Though she lost, she pushed into the top 10 of the World Tennis Association rankings for the first time since Olympia's birth.

Nadia Comăneci

BE **BRAVE**—IN SPORTS AND IN LIFE

When Nadia Comăneci was six years old in 1968, she was chosen to attend one of the most selective gymnastics schools in the Soviet Union, which was run by coach Béla Károlyi in her home country of Romania. Nadia took to gymnastics immediately. "I was a true tomboy," she wrote in her autobiography, "with uncontrollable energy that at times pushed my parents to the limits." She'd spend hours jumping on beds, running around her village, and trying to play with the little boys who lived nearby. It made sense that she'd love a sport that demanded as much physical energy as gymnastics.

After training for six hours a day, five days a week, Nadia won the Romanian nationals event when she was just nine, and four years later, when she was 13, she stole the show at the European Women's Artistic Gymnastics Championships in Norway. There, she won the all-around gold medal as well as gold medals in every event but the floor exercise, where she placed second. That was a year before the 1976 Olympics in Montreal, and Nadia went from being just another promising young gymnast to being a favorite to win.

She was just 14 when she arrived in Canada for the Games, and she was awestruck by the Olympic village and the excitement in the air. She discovered peanut butter, pizza, and cereal, none of which she'd ever seen before. Coming from the closed-off Soviet Union, she hadn't realized what a spectacle she was walking into—but she made history almost immediately. Competing on the uneven bars, Nadia scored a perfect 10, moving effortlessly between the two bars without a single mistake. Her body was totally controlled at all times and her dismount flawless. The scoreboard in Montreal wasn't even programmed to display a double-digit number, the perfect "10" that she had earned! As a result, it displayed a "1.00."

> ❝WHEN I MAKE A DECISION, I DON'T DOUBT IT. **I GO ALL THE WAY HOPING THAT IT IS GOING TO BE GOOD.**❞

Nadia would go on to amaze the judges and confound the scoreboard six more times during those Olympics, winning three gold medals: in uneven bars, balance beam, and all-around. Four of Nadia's seven perfect scores came on the uneven bars. The other three 10s came on the balance beam, where her excellent balance and strong, confident hand placement wowed judges. Nadia told Euronews, "I think that you have to work hard to be up to that level. I think I am not looking for the easy way to do things, and I am proud about that."

While Nadia's career took off, she faced tough conditions in her home country, which was part of the tightly controlled Soviet Union. The Romanian government had interfered in Nadia's career, forcing her to leave her beloved coaches and work with a different coaching staff for a year between 1977 and 1978. During that time, she struggled. She grew taller and gained a bit of weight, and she had to adjust her approach without her trusted coaches. Still, at the 1980 Olympics in Moscow, Nadia won two gold medals and two silvers. (The United States boycotted the Olympics that year, angry at the

Soviet government because it invaded Afghanistan.)

In 1981, Nadia was back working with Károlyi and his wife, Márta, and she was sent along with them on a tour of the United States. This was big news in the middle of the Cold War, the decades-long conflict between the U.S. and other democratic nations and the Soviet Union, which lasted from 1947 until 1991. Citizens of the Soviet Union were closely monitored and not allowed to move out of the country, but during the trip, the Károlyis managed to slip away, remaining in the United States to improve their quality of life. Nadia wasn't ready to make such a drastic decision when her coaches did, and she returned to Romania.

Three years later, while in California to observe the Los Angeles Olympics, Nadia was forbidden to talk to her former coaches. Back in Romania, life was getting harder. Basic goods like gas and food were hard to come by, and Nadia's government kept a close eye on her. Eventually, she'd had enough and devised a plan to escape. One night in November 1989, Nadia joined a group of Romanians and a guide and traveled on foot across the border into Hungary, a six-hour journey through mud and across frozen rivers. It was a huge risk, but they made their way to Austria, where they boarded a plane to the United States. "I made a very bold decision at that time because I knew it was very dangerous and scary," Nadia said of leaving Romania, "but . . . like in gymnastics, I liked to try new skills."

Nadia has lived in America ever since. After the fall of the Soviet Union in the 1990s, she began to spend time in Romania again, opening a free medical clinic for children in 2009, and later bringing her son to visit his grandparents. She and her husband, Olympic gymnast Bart Conner, are devoted supporters of the Special Olympics, and run a gymnastics academy in Oklahoma, where perhaps they will train the next Nadia.

Lizzie Armanto

STAND UP TO BULLIES

In 2007, when Lizzie Armanto was 14 and living in California, she and her younger brother decided to check out the local skateboarding scene. They learned how to skate in bowls, which look like giant empty swimming pools with sloped sides, and on verts, which are above-ground ramps where skateboarders speed up and down inclines, moving faster and faster as they travel back and forth, sometimes spinning in the air at the top. Lizzie was especially talented, though at first, her only goal was to be better than her brother.

Quickly, skateboarding became more than just a hobby for the teenager. By 2010, three years after she started taking skateboarding seriously, Lizzie was racking up points in the World Cup of Skateboarding, the organization that hosts skateboarding competitions and rewards athletes with points for wins. The bigger the win and more prestigious the event, the more points a skater earns. In fact, few people were earning points as fast as Lizzie, and from 2010 to 2012, she earned more points than any other skateboarder. In 2013, she competed in the X Games for the first time, in Barcelona, and there she finished first in the women's skateboarding event, becoming the youngest woman to medal in X Games history. Throughout the event, Lizzie focused on McTwists, the difficult move in which a skater does a front flip while rotating 1.5 times. They're one of the toughest feats in the sport, and Lizzie knew if she could pull them off, she'd be in great shape to medal. She did. In her next X Games appearance three years later, she placed second, and she followed that up with sixth, seventh, and third place finishes over the next three years.

In 2018, Lizzie's biggest news came not at the X Games, but on an eight-foot-wide ramp owned by legendary skateboarder Tony Hawk. Called The Loop, it's a 360-degree ramp that looks like a curly-cue, with a 14-foot drop. Skateboarders start out skating down a small ramp to gain speed. The ramp flattens out, and then it becomes an incline, going up and over in a circular shape so skaterboarders are briefly upside down. Once they've gone all the way around, they coast on a flat surface out of The Loop. Hawk was able to complete The Loop during his career, but stopped trying now that he's retired. He'd injured himself on too many attempts.

When Lizzie got a chance to master the ramp, she made the most of it. She gave The Loop a chance one day, when other skaters were taking practice sessions on it, with giant pads pushed onto the bottom of The Loop to help skaters land painlessly if they crashed. The pads would prevent them from actually completing the trick, but they were great for extra practice reps, so Lizzie knew she'd have to come back the next day to give it a try with just the hard, solid ground beneath her. When she returned, she tried The Loop over and over for five hours, falling on her black kneepads every time she tried to stick the landing. Eventually, though, she executed it perfectly, coasting out of the 360-degree rotation to applause. "It was crazy," Lizzie told PopSugar.com. "I

> **"A BIG PART OF TRYING IS JUST GOING FOR IT. EVERYONE HAS TO START SOMEWHERE."**

didn't know I actually made it through until I was halfway across the parking lot [afterwards]." Fewer than 20 people in the world have successfully completed The Loop, and Lizzie was the first woman to ever land it. As a result of her talent there and in competitions across the world, Lizzie was made into a playable character in two Tony Hawk video games: *Shred Session* and *Pro Skater 5*. She plans to appear on even more screens in Tokyo at the 2021 Olympics, too. Lizzie will be competing for the Finnish team (she holds dual citizenship because her father was born in Finland). It's a huge reward for a skater who's trained so intensely for more than a decade, skating so fearlessly that she once knocked out her teeth during a bad landing. "I knew exactly what had happened," Lizzie told *Thrasher* magazine. "It was weird 'cause it was one of the hardest slams I've taken, but breaking your teeth doesn't really hurt that much."

Lizzie has also become active in promoting other girls, encouraging them to get involved in skateboarding, and combating bullying within the sport. In 2019, she collaborated with other skateboarders and two directors to star in a video that shows the public the kind of harassment that female skateboarders have to deal with on social media. In the video, Lizzie skateboards down a sidewalk and through a tunnel, showing off her skills while a male voice reads pieces of criticism that she's gotten on social media: that a young boy could do better, that she wouldn't get the same attention for her skills if she were a boy, that she's only celebrated for her looks, not her talent. "These words represent the darkest side of skateboarding," Lizzie wrote on Instagram when she posted the video. "We wanted to illuminate these grotesque comments with hopes of drawing attention to the issue. The skateboarding community is a vibrant collective of individuals with the capacity to eradicate such hate. Let us work together to rise up and support every skateboarder, no matter their gender, orientation, or race."

Michelle Wie

CARVE YOUR OWN
PATH TO SUCCESS

Michelle Wie was a child prodigy. She picked up golf not long after she learned to run, hitting her first balls when she was just four years old under her mother's supervision. In her tiny swing, her parents and golf professionals saw something, and Michelle loved the sport so much that she began to train seriously at a young age.

When she was 10, Michelle became the youngest girl to ever qualify for the U.S. Women's Amateur tournament and for any Ladies Professional Golf Association (LPGA) event. When she was 11, she got two huge wins, both at respected tournaments in her home state of Hawaii. The next year, she proved how far ahead of the rest of the field she was when she won the Hawaii State Open Women's Division tournament by 13 shots. It was a blowout, and it looked a lot like there would be more of those in Michelle's future.

At age 13, Michelle took the golf world by storm, when she made the cut at her first U.S. Women's Open tournament, at Orchards Golf Club in Massachusetts. (The cut comes after the first two days of the tournament, when about half of the golfers are eliminated and the top half plays on.) Just a middle schooler, she was on national television being praised as the youngest girl to ever play on Saturday and Sunday at the U.S. Women's Open. Though she fell off from her leaderboard position from the earlier rounds (she was four strokes off the lead at the end of the second day of play), just having Michelle at the tournament drew fans to the course in droves.

LPGA rules state that a golfer must be 18 to qualify as a professional on the tour, but Michelle decided to turn pro a week before her 16th birthday. She was famous and wildly popular among fans, and becoming a professional meant she could profit from her success. Until she turned 18, though, she was limited to competing in eight LPGA tournaments per year. So for the first two years of her pro career, she had to find tournaments outside of the LPGA tour as she brought in money from sponsors like Nike and Sony, who knew Michelle would be a star.

> **"YOU NEED TO ENVISION THE PERFECT SHOT ON EVERY HOLE, AND MOST OF THE TIME, IT DOESN'T END UP THAT WAY."**

Scheduling was tricky. Michelle competed in as many LPGA tournaments as she could, but she began to get an even more interesting opportunity: to play against men. Michelle received invitations to play in elite men's tournaments, and fans were eager to see how she'd do there against bigger and stronger competition. Often, she was able to drive the ball farther than men whose biceps appeared to be twice the size of hers, causing the jaws of spectators across the course to drop. Still, Michelle missed the cut in all but one of those men's tournaments and descended into a slump.

In 2008, a year after she'd enrolled at Stanford University, Michelle stopped competing in men's tournaments. Since she was a professional golfer, earning money for wins and endorsements, she couldn't play for Stanford's team, but she applied herself to her studies while still traveling to golf tournaments around the world. She was determined to get an education and to continue to improve her game. And she knew that when she graduated, she would be able to dedicate herself 100% to the sport she loved.

While in college, Michelle won her first two tournaments, one in 2009 and another the next year. The 2010 win, at the CN Canadian Open, was one of the highlights of her young LPGA career. Tall and skinny, wearing a pink skirt and white shirt, Michelle teed off on the par-3 11th hole, eyeing the green. She swung, watched her ball arc through the air, land, and roll right into the hole for an ace. A year before, she'd had another hole-in-one, the first of her pro career, and she'd danced to celebrate. This time, she just smiled, and the shot widened her lead at the tournament she'd eventually win by three strokes.

After graduating college, Michelle won her third LPGA event in 2014, which was shaping up to be the biggest year of her career. Eleven years after she first made the cut at the U.S. Women's Open, Michelle won the event. At 24 years old, she was the only woman to shoot a score under par for the tournament. "If I won it [when I was younger] I would have been like, 'Oh, cool, this is awesome,'" Wie said after winning. "But I think it means a lot more to me because I went through so much."

HOW MICHELLE GETS HER GROOVE BACK

Michelle's late teens and early 20s were a tough time in her career. She was no longer the youngest player on tour, nor was she winning events like she used to, and she had to balance school at Stanford with her professional career. To help her rebound, she focused on her hobbies, like cooking and painting. She also developed a deep love of fashion. "I feel like my hobbies outside of golf keep me sane, and it keeps me feeling like I'm normal," Michelle told Golf.com. In college, she also fell in love with drawing after a close friend sent her a sketch pad and crayons. At first, Michelle was skeptical, but then she turned on the creative portion of her brain and began to make colorful masterpieces of everything from robots to people to butterflies. "When I'm drawing, the rest of the world disappears," Michelle told the *New York Times*. "I think it just makes me really happy. It takes my mind off of things. When I'm stressed out, it's like a positive outlet I can go to relieve stress. It puts me in a better mood."

Gertrude Ederle

IF AT FIRST YOU DON'T SUCCEED. . .

When American swimmer Gertrude Ederle prepared to swim 35 miles across the English Channel in 1926, most of the world was convinced she couldn't do it. Gertrude was a celebrated swimmer—she'd won a gold medal in the 4x100-meter freestyle relay, along with two bronze medals in individual events, at the Olympics in Paris in 1924. No one questioned that Gertrude was one of the world's best swimmers. What they did say, however, was that no *woman* would be able to make it across the Channel.

Gertrude fueled that argument in 1925, when she tried the swim unsuccessfully—which wasn't entirely her fault. When Gertrude was out in the open water, her coach saw her coughing and was worried she was going under, so he reached out to help her, invalidating the attempt. That was only a setback, though, and Gertrude continued to train in open-water swimming for another year, until the heat of the summer in 1926. On August 6, she dove into the chilly ocean again and began to paddle in her signature fashion—freestyle, with eight kicks for every arm stroke—and this time, she kept swimming . . . and swimming, and swimming.

Fourteen hours and 31 minutes after she left Dover, England, Gertrude made it safely to shore at Cape Gris-Nez, France. Yes, a woman could swim across the Channel—and she could do it faster than the fastest man, it turned out. With her time, Gertrude set a new record for the Channel swim, breaking the previous one by nearly two hours.

A year after failing, she made the swim look easy, in large part because she adjusted after her first attempt. In the 1920s, women wore heavy one-piece bathing suits, and Gertrude realized her old suit had weighed her down. Her solution? She took scissors to her swimsuit, cutting it into a two-piece, which made it much lighter and caused it to drag less in the waves. From there, she slathered her body in grease to help her glide through the water and to protect her against cold temperatures and jellyfish stings. Gertrude also studied the tides more on her second attempt, leaving at precisely the right time. She also made sure the support boat that followed her from England to France was properly stocked with chicken legs, oranges, and soup to keep her energized. She also wore a large pair of goggles that looked more like those a skier would wear today than anything seen in the pool—but they did the trick.

The press, most of it dismissive of her quest, still turned out to see how far Gertrude might make it. They set sail alongside her support boat, using radios to broadcast her progress across the world. Newspapers published breathless updates when she finished, though it was tough for her to give interviews. The swim was exhausting. She emerged from the water covered in jellyfish stings. Her face was bruised from the waves, and her tongue was so swollen from exposure to saltwater that she could barely speak.

SWIM LIKE GERTRUDE!

Every fall in New York, brave swimmers can sign up for the annual Ederle-Burke Swim, which is named for Gertrude and another swimmer, Eileen Burke. Its route goes from Battery Park in Manhattan to Sandy Hook, New Jersey, and swimmers pass the Statue of Liberty, Ellis Island, and the Verrazzano-Narrows Bridge. According to Gertrude's family members, she swam this route in 1925 as a warm-up for her Channel swim, finishing it in seven hours and 11 minutes.

For a time, Gertrude was one of the most famous athletes in the world. She received a ticker-tape parade in New York when she returned to the United States, and President Calvin Coolidge dubbed her "America's best girl." Gertrude's record held until 1951, when another woman, Winnie Roach-Leuszler, topped it.

Eventually, Gertrude's tongue returned to its normal size, and her bruises faded. But the swim had one long-lasting effect: Gertrude had already suffered from hearing loss due to a childhood illness, and the swim permanently worsened her hearing. She became partially deaf, but she got on with her swimming career until 1933, when she fell down a flight of stairs and injured her back so severely doctors told her she would never walk or swim again.

Gertrude was able to slowly rehabilitate from her back injury over the course of the 1930s. In 1939, she got back in the swimming business, taking part in Billy Rose's Aquacade, an aquatics show at the New York World's Fair. Inspired by her own impaired hearing, she also decided to work closely with deaf children to help them learn and excel at her sport. In 1978, the pool where she competed on the Upper West Side of Manhattan was dedicated in her name.

the Gertrude Ederle INDOOR POOL

"TO ME, **THE SEA IS LIKE A PERSON**—LIKE A CHILD THAT I'VE KNOWN A LONG TIME."

Ibtihaj Muhammad

BECOME THE ROLE MODEL

When Ibtihaj Muhammad was a little girl, her mother made her special outfits for all of her sporting events. An African American Muslim, Ibtihaj had begun wearing a hijab—the traditional Muslim headscarf—at a young age, and most sports uniforms were too revealing for the standards her religion imposed. That's where her mother's sewing skills came in handy, and Ibtihaj was able to compete in volleyball, swimming, tennis, softball, and track. She wore homemade uniforms that covered her arms and legs and "allowed her to participate while still being true to her faith," her mother, Denise, told ESPN in 2011.

When Ibtihaj (pronounced Ib-tee-haj, though she often goes by the nickname Ibti) was 13, she joined the fencing team at her high school in New Jersey. Because fencing is a combat sport based on sword fighting, all fencers must wear a protective costume, which includes long sleeves, pants, and a screen-like mask that covers their heads and faces. Fencing, then, was the first sport Ibtihaj played in which she didn't have to modify her uniform. All she had to do was pop her mask over her hijab, and she was ready to go. That wouldn't have been the case in many other sports if Ibtihaj had wanted to play at a high level. In fact, FIFA, soccer's governing body, didn't allow women to wear hijabs until 2014, and the International Volleyball Federation forced beach players to wear bikinis until 2012.

From the start of her career, Ibtihaj was one of very few people of color competing in fencing. Even fewer wore hijabs. She was accustomed to living in a world where others didn't look like her, and she had plenty of practice improvising. As a girl, Ibtihaj had played with brown-skinned Barbies almost exclusively, but when she began wearing her hijab, she felt that even they didn't represent her—but rather than accept that, she began to make hijabs for her dolls out of small pieces of fabric.

By the end of high school, Ibtihaj focused on fencing and left other sports behind. With her speed and strength, she earned a scholarship to compete at Duke University in the sabre division of the sport.

There are three types of sword used in fencing—foil, épée, and sabre—and the rules for competing are a little bit different depending on the weapon the fencer uses. In sabre fencing, athletes use the edges and backs of their blades, rather than just the points, to hit.

Wearing her hijab to compete on bigger and bigger stages, Ibtihaj was proud to provide an example to girls around the world that they could do whatever they dreamed of while wearing their headscarves. When she finished college, she wanted to continue working at the sport she loved. Her goal was to make the U.S. national team. With that in mind, she began to train in Manhattan with some of the best in the game, living at home and pinching pennies to help fund her dream.

"IN A WAY, MY LIFE AND MY JOURNEY HAVE ALWAYS BEEN BIGGER THAN FENCING. COMPETING AT THE OLYMPICS WAS ALSO ABOUT RESHAPING THE NARRATIVE AROUND WHO A MUSLIM WOMAN IS: WHAT SHE LOOKS LIKE, WHAT SHE DOES."

In 2010, that decision paid off. Ibtihaj became a member of the United States National Fencing Team, and though she missed the Olympics in 2012, she was on top of her game by 2016, when she qualified to compete in Rio de Janeiro. There, she became the first Muslim woman to wear a hijab while competing for the United States in the Olympics. She earned a bronze medal in the team sabre competition, where groups of four teammates go head-to-head with other countries. The United States team lost in the semifinal round to Russia but won the third-place match, thanks in large part to Ibtihaj's aggressive play. When she collected her bronze, she became the first Muslim American woman to win a medal at the Games. It reminded her of how difficult her road to the Olympics was and how lonely she sometimes felt. "There were no role models," Ibtihaj told the *New Yorker.* "When I competed in local tournaments, there were often comments about me—being Black, or being Muslim. It hurt."

But her love for the sport drove her, and she continued to compete. In 2017, she was ranked the No. 2 woman fencer in the United States, No. 7 in the World. That same year, Mattel introduced its first hijab-wearing Barbie. It was modeled after Ibtihaj. Girls who come after her will no longer have to resort to sewing scraps of fabric to feel connected to their favorite dolls.

CALMING PRE-GAME NERVES

For most athletes, competition can bring out the jitters. The anticipation of games, tournaments, and all kinds of sports matches can lead to nerves, and Ibtihaj has figured out how to recognize when her body is reacting to stress, as well as how to calm herself down. "The morning of a competition I'd wake up feeling lethargic and sleepy—overwhelmingly so—despite having had a good night's rest," she told *Glamour.* "At game time I'd [go] onto the fencing strip and feel completely detached from reality." Ibtihaj also said that she sometimes felt like her arms and legs were "made of lead." Those feelings led her to see a sports psychologist, who helped her develop healthy coping mechanisms so that she could start feeling more like herself before big competitions. Through prayer and meditation, she's learned how to ground herself and become her "own best cheerleader."

Naomi Osaka

STAY **TRUE** TO YOUR HERITAGE

Naomi Osaka was born halfway across the world from the United States, in the city of Osaka in Southern Japan. Her mother, Tamaki, is Japanese, and her father, Leonard, is Haitian. When her family moved to New York, her parents held tight to the cultures that shaped them.

Naomi was just three when she arrived in America, and she grew up immersed in both Haitian and Japanese traditions. Her mother often spoke in her native language, and her father's parents, who lived in New York, spoke Creole. Naomi's home was a melting pot, and she and her older sister, Mari, identify as both Black and Asian. "I've never really fit into one description—but people are so fast to give me a label. *Is she Japanese? American? Haitian? Black? Asian?*" Naomi wrote in an essay in *Esquire* in 2020. "Well, I'm all of these things together at the same time."

When Naomi was very young, her father began to watch tennis, and he noticed two women who looked nothing like most of the world's top players: Venus and Serena Williams (see page 56). They were winning Grand Slams and signing endorsement deals in a historically white sport. Tennis was changing. Why couldn't Naomi and Mari become just as talented and just as famous?

The Williams sisters had learned tennis from their father, and so would the Osaka girls. Though Leonard had never played the sport, he followed Richard Williams's example, teaching his daughters

"AS LONG AS I CAN REMEMBER, PEOPLE HAVE STRUGGLED TO **DEFINE** ME."

everything they needed to learn to be successful. The girls were naturals, especially Naomi, and when she was nine, the family packed its bags again, this time for Florida. Leonard wanted his daughters to have every resource imaginable, and Florida was a hotbed of tennis talent.

On her 14th birthday, Naomi played in her first ITF Women's World Tennis Tour event. When she was 15, she turned pro and began to play in tournaments all around the world, including one in Japan. As Naomi kept playing, she continued to rise in the World Tennis Association rankings. In 2016, she was named the WTA Newcomer of the Year, and in 2018, she won her first Grand Slam, the US Open, where she defeated Serena Williams in the final.

In 2019, Naomi won the Australian Open and became the top-ranked women's player in the world, making history when she got there; no Asian woman had ever before been ranked No. 1. That year, Naomi also had a decision to make. She'd begun to train and plan for the Olympics, which were supposed to be held in Tokyo in 2020, but were rescheduled for 2021. Naomi held dual citizenship in Japan and the United States, and she decided to represent Japan at the Games. "It is a special feeling to aim for the Olympics as a representative of Japan," she told NHK, a Japanese broadcasting company. "I think that playing with the pride of the country will make me feel more emotional."

As she traveled the world competing, Naomi became one of the most famous players in all of tennis winning huge endorsement deals. Barbie even made a doll that looked like her. But one of her highlights of 2019 actually came off the court, when she flew to Haiti for a visit. There, the country's president and prime minister welcomed her and threw a parade in her honor. She was given a key to the city of

Jacmel, where her father was born. She also visited an elementary school that her family funded, and while she was there, she made a big announcement: She promised to donate all the money she made from her Barbie to the school, to help it expand and even build tennis courts. She hoped to share her favorite sport with children in her father's home country, where 65% of the population lives in poverty.

"It helped me be grateful that I'm even on the court, that I'm not injured, having the opportunity to play the matches," Naomi told the *Miami Herald* about her visit. "Little things I used to complain about definitely are not a big deal to me anymore. Even if I lose, I realize this isn't the worst thing that could happen to me."

Once she returned to the United States, Naomi didn't stop speaking up about inequalities. When a Minneapolis police officer murdered George Floyd in May of 2020, Naomi knew she needed to do something. She flew to Minneapolis in the days after Floyd's death and joined in peaceful protests. "I kept asking myself what can I do to make this world a better place for my children?" Naomi wrote. "I decided it was time to speak up about systemic racism and police brutality."

And that's what she's been doing ever since: investing in communities, peacefully protesting, speaking out. When tennis competition resumed later that summer, Naomi made a statement at the US Open, wearing a new and different face mask in every round. Each had the name of a Black victim of racial injustice on it. From Breonna Taylor in the first round to Tamir Rice in the final, Naomi made a statement each time she picked up her racket—and then she won the tournament, too.

In the 2021 French Open, she made her biggest statement yet—by withdrawing. After being criticized and penalized for declining to give media interviews during the tournament, she announced that she would be tending to her mental health—proving once again that she knows exactly what matters most.

Mia Hamm

DON'T APOLOGIZE **FOR AMBITION**

When Mia Hamm was a toddler, she was diagnosed with a partial club foot and forced to wear corrective shoes. At 18 months old, her foot in the midst of being treated, she saw a family kicking a soccer ball outdoors. Instead of just observing, though, she ran after them and kicked the ball as hard as she could.

That was the day the greatest women's soccer player of her generation discovered her favorite sport. It didn't take long for Mia to start playing the game in a more organized fashion rather than by stealing another family's equipment. When she was five, her foot now corrected, she joined her first team in Wichita Falls, Texas, where she was raised. Mia was talented and willing to put in the work, both in soccer and other sports, too. In fact, she loved athletics so much that she played on her junior high's football team as a wide receiver and defensive back. She also idolized stars outside of soccer, including Jackie Joyner-Kersee in track and field (see page 142) and Chris Evert in tennis.

Soon, though, it was time to specialize in soccer, and when Mia was just 15, she joined the U.S. women's national team as the youngest member in its history. Two years later, she enrolled at the University of North Carolina to play college soccer and impressed coaches early with the training routine she brought with her. Not only did Mia go all-out in the team's practices, but she could also be found running wind sprints alone—anything to improve her game and make

"IT'S TIME TO BREAK THIS STEREOTYPE OF THE PASSIVE WOMAN, AND ONE OF THE BEST WAYS I CAN THINK OF TO DO THIS IS TO RAISE A RUCKUS WHEN YOU STICK THE BALL IN THE BACK OF THE NET."

her more dominant at her position, forward. "There is no substitute for hard work," Mia said. "A consistent work ethic will benefit you in all aspects of life, and you are letting your teammates down when you do not push yourself to be your best."

While at UNC, Mia helped lead the Tar Heels to four consecutive national championships. She also spent time away, competing with the national team, which won the World Cup in 1991. Still the youngest player on the squad, Mia scored the game-winning goal against Sweden in the second half of their first match in the tournament. It was her first taste of victory on an international stage. The U.S. came in third in her next World Cup in 1995. Something even bigger loomed, though: the Olympics. In 1996 in Atlanta, the Games would feature women's soccer for the first time, and Mia was the star of the U.S. women's team, which had a great shot for a medal. At 24, Mia was confident and unapologetic that she wanted nothing more than to win. "I learned to embrace the fact that I loved to compete," she said. "I found a comfort in training beside and competing with my teammates on the National Team, which was the first group of women that I was able to share that experience with in my life. Girls should never apologize for wanting to be great."

At the Olympics, the U.S. women cruised to the final game, which was against China, the team they'd tied earlier in the tournament. Mia battled nagging injuries throughout the Olympics, though. She hurt her foot in a game against Sweden and then her groin in practice the day before the final game. In the final, Mia played a huge part in the U.S.'s first goal (Shannon MacMillan scored by tapping in a rebound of Mia's deflected shot), but when the game was tied at halftime, she worried that her injuries might be dragging the team down. She offered to sit out. The rest of the women disagreed and urged her to keep playing if she could. Mia stayed in, and her pass helped set up what would be the game-winning goal for the U.S., though Mia wasn't on the field when the clock stopped. She'd been carried to the sideline on a stretcher a minute earlier, exhausted and worn down by her injuries. Still, she was able to hobble over to join the celebrations.

Mia would go on to win an Olympic silver medal four years later and another gold four years after that. Her team won the World Cup again in 1999 and placed third in 2003, with Mia as the biggest name on each of those rosters. By the time she retired in 2004, she'd set a new record for the most international goals scored by a woman or a man, and she'd been the biggest star in the U.S.'s first-ever women's professional soccer league. She finished her soccer career on top, a winner at every level earning a place in the National Women's Hall of Fame in 2021. "Take your victories, whatever they may be, cherish them, use them, but don't settle for them," Mia wrote in her book, *Go For the Goal*. "There are always new, grander challenges to confront, and a true winner will embrace each one."

TAKE TIME FOR YOURSELF

Like most star athletes, her sport was her life, and it involved hours and hours of training each week, everything from sprints to stair runs to weightlifting. But Mia learned that sometimes, the best way to prepare for a big game is to chill out. "Remember to take time for yourself," she wrote in her autobiography. "The real winners have balance in their lives. When training camp gets too intense, I recommend doing what we do—goof off. That means playing hearts for Oreo cookies, cruising the local mall, and watching a tape of any Adam Sandler movie." By taking that time away from the gym or the soccer field, Mia allowed herself to have a mental break and to remember the best part of the game: fun.

Kendall Coyne Schofield

MAKE YOUR OWN FUTURE

When Kendall Coyne Schofield was a senior forward on Northeastern University's hockey team in 2016, she was awarded the highest honor in women's college hockey: the Patty Kazmaier Award, which recognizes the best player in the sport. That year, she'd been a team captain and led Northeastern to its first NCAA tournament appearance ever. Kendall also scored more goals than any other woman in college that season, finishing with 50. She was at the top of her game, looking forward to playing hockey after graduation.

Growing up in the Chicago area, Kendall was a strong all-around athlete. She started skating when she was three years old and her brother began to play hockey. Though she loved nothing more than to lace up her skates, Kendall competed in two sports, softball and ice hockey, until her sophomore year of high school. She believes that continuing with softball for so long ultimately helped her enjoy and excel at hockey even more. "In hockey, I was the only girl on the team for a long time," she told admkids.com. "Softball was that balance that helped me meet other girls in sports." It was also a change of pace that kept her from getting burnt out on a single sport—but hockey was her obsession. "I loved the game, and that's why I shot pucks in my basement, everywhere, did sit-ups and push-ups," Kendall said, recalling her childhood. She showed exceptional talent from almost the minute she picked up a stick, and she attended the Berkshire School, a prep school with a strong hockey team. From there, it was an easy transition to Northeastern.

Kendall never had to think about the next steps of her hockey career: there had always been the next level of a club team, then prep school, then college. At Northeastern, though, the path became complicated. When Kendall started college, there was no women's professional hockey league in the United States. The only way to keep playing after graduation would be to make the Olympic team— which has just 23 spots. "If you're not one of the 23," she said, "then that's it?"

In 2014, Kendall was one of the 23, and she took the season off from playing at Northeastern to train with the U.S. women's national team. That winter, she flew to Sochi, Russia, and won a silver medal at her first Olympics.

A year later, when Kendall was finishing her third season on the ice at college, another Northeastern alumna founded the National Women's Hockey League (NWHL). Kendall was picked third overall in the league's first draft, thanks to her explosive speed and tenacity. Kendall has always been known as the speediest woman on the ice, moving swiftly—not just in a straight line but also around quick defenders, leaving them in her icy trail. That skill appealed to many people in the NWHL who dreamed of having Kendall on their team for the league's first season.

But Kendall had a year of eligibility at Northeastern remaining, meaning that she could play another season and work on a master's degree. Though being sought after by the NWHL was an honor, she was uncertain about the new league and its ability to pay players adequately, so she

> **"WE SEE LITTLE GIRLS NOW WHO WANT TO BE HOCKEY PLAYERS BECAUSE THEY LOVE HOCKEY, NOT BECAUSE THEIR BROTHERS PLAYED."**

stayed in school, securing her legacy and arming herself with her education.

After graduating, Kendall decided the NWHL wasn't for her. The league had cut salaries, and she figured she'd be better off playing with an independent hockey team, the Minnesota Whitecaps. Minnesota couldn't pay Kendall, but competing wasn't a full-time commitment. She split her time between Minnesota, Denver (where her fiancé played in the NFL), and Chicago (where she had a job that provided her income). When the Whitecaps joined the NWHL in 2018, Kendall signed with them again, helping lead the team to the NWHL championship in their very first year. She also competed in her second Olympics in 2018, winning gold in Pyeongchang, South Korea, by defeating Canada in a shoot-out. It was the first time the U.S. women had won gold on the ice in 20 years.

Back home, even with medals in hand, it was still hard for the women to find professional success on the ice. The NWHL wasn't paying players enough to live on, so Kendall and others formed a union and sat out the 2019-20 season in a protest for better salaries. Even so, Kendall was never far from the rink.

She competed in the skills challenge at the NHL All-Star Game in 2019 against some of the fastest skaters in the NHL and held her own—finishing not even a second behind the speediest man. Kendall returned to the All-Star event in 2020, participating as part of an all-woman 3-on-3 tournament. It was the highest-profile women's event yet at an NHL All-Star weekend, and though Canada defeated Kendall's American team, all the women on the ice were ready to celebrate the fact that the game even took place as a victory. In front of thousands of fans, they'd gotten to showcase their speed, passing abilities, and powerful shots. In 2021, Kendall made history one more time, becoming the first female assistant coach for the Rockford IceHogs.

Jessica Mendoza

SHOW WHAT **YOU** KNOW

When Jessica Mendoza was a little girl playing softball on teams coached by local parents, she began to notice a trend: her dad and other dads would coach the girls, but the moms never seemed to cross over and work with the boys' baseball teams.

That was just the reality, but Jessica loved any sport where she could hit balls with bats. As she grew older, she knew that meant she'd be a softball player. Girls didn't play baseball, and so Jessica learned a game with a larger, softer ball that's thrown underhand, rather than overhand like in baseball. She was great at it—so good that she earned a scholarship to Stanford University to play in the outfield. Jessica arrived there in 1999 and immediately made a huge impact. As a freshman, she broke school records for batting average and runs batted in. The next year, she was named the conference's best player, and she broke her own batting average record with the best mark of her career, hitting .474. In fact, no other college softball player had a better average than Jessica that year.

Opposing pitchers knew Jessica was the player to fear on Stanford's roster, and at one point during her sophomore season, she got a hit in 19 consecutive games. The next year, as a junior, she helped power Stanford to the Women's College World Series for the first time in school history. Her senior season, she tied her own home run record and continued to be one of the best hitters in all of college softball.

When Jessica finished college, she joined the United States national softball team, winning a gold medal at the 2003 Pan American Games. She played in her first Olympics in 2004, winning a gold medal and scoring five runs over the course of the tournament. Four years later, she and the U.S. women won a silver medal in Beijing, and in a crucial game during those Olympics, Jessica hit three home runs and drove in four runs against the Chinese Taipei team.

> **"REMEMBER WHO YOU ARE AND WHAT MAKES YOU GOOD.** WHAT DO YOU DO BEST? STICK WITH THAT."**

Between international competitions, Jessica played in the National Pro Fastpitch softball league. During the time she competed professionally there, she had a baby, went on maternity leave, and quickly returned to form as a great hitter. When it was time to retire, Jessica joined ESPN in 2007, and as a rookie broadcaster, she had a lot to learn. That didn't bother her, though. As a young girl, Jessica had let ball after ball roll through her legs into the outfield, and she'd struck out often as she gradually took to softball. It took time and patience to build her skills on the diamond, so she knew that if she put her mind to television, she could become a star there, too. At ESPN, Jessica started out covering softball, college baseball, and college football. As she moved through the ranks at the network, she found herself spending more and more time in the world of baseball—in part because ESPN spends so much time covering the sport. She was one of the few women in the roles she filled, but that rarely bothered her. "I've been the girl always trying to play with the boys, you know?" she told NPR. "I played baseball with all boys. They didn't want to play catch with me. I mean, it's the story of everything I've done."

Jessica made history in 2015, when she became the first woman in the broadcast booth for the College World Series. She then became the first woman to serve as a commentator at a Major League Baseball game on ESPN just two months later, when she called a game between the Cardinals and the Diamondbacks. She was filling in for retired pitcher Curt Schilling that evening, and she substituted again six days later on *Sunday Night Baseball* for a game between the Cubs and the Dodgers. That night, she ended up calling a no-hitter. Jessica continued to impress, explaining pitch sequencing (how pitchers decide what to throw, and in what order) and the mechanics of hitting to viewers. She was on the broadcast again for the American League Wild Card Game that fall, making her the first woman ever to be a commentator in postseason history. "You know, I wasn't even thinking about my gender or anything," she said. "I literally was so in tune with the game."

Still, Jessica received plenty of blowback from baseball fans who didn't think a woman belonged in the broadcast booth. Instead of worrying about them, she continued to provide smart analysis on air, proving she knew baseball inside and out.

Jessica joined the *Sunday Night Baseball* team full-time the next year, which was a huge promotion to one of the highest-profile broadcast teams in all of sports. The ESPN Sunday night game is the only one played in that time slot each week, and viewers from across the country tune in. Today, she continues to work as a baseball analyst for ESPN. She also spent a year serving as an advisor to the Mets. Three decades after Jessica noticed that women couldn't quite crack into baseball, she did—showing fans and MLB leadership that a softball player can have just as sharp of a mind for the game of baseball as anyone who's played the men's sport.

Laila Ali

CREATE YOUR **OWN** LEGACY

When Laila Ali was a little girl, boxing was nothing more than the sport her famous father, Muhammad Ali, had dominated. Laila didn't have much interest in it, and she didn't even know women's boxing existed. She dreamed of becoming a manicurist, and despite getting in trouble as a child—she did a stint in juvenile detention for shoplifting—Laila had the discipline to take the bus to and from a cosmetology program while she was still in high school.

By the time Laila was 18, she was an entrepreneur with plans to go to business school. She owned her own nail salon and had been doing nails professionally for three years. Then, she watched Christy Martin, the first woman to have a long and successful boxing career in the United States, fight. While she couldn't quite get it out of her mind, she also knew that entering that world would not be easy for her. "I thought of all the attention that would be on me and all the pressure—my dad's legacy and coming behind him and what that would mean," Laila told ESPN. "Would I be able to deal with it? It took me about a year of contemplation, and I decided to go for it."

Laila was determined to find her own place in the boxing world. She trained in secret before announcing her decision on *Good Morning America*. And though boxing fans were excited to see her in the ring, her father was not. He worried about how dangerous boxing can be, and he didn't want his daughter to get hurt. Still, Laila pressed on. In 1999, at age 21, she made her debut before a crowd of fans and journalists. Against an inexperienced boxer, she won in just 31 seconds. Her second opponent, another boxer who'd just turned professional, lost to Laila, too. In fact, Laila kept winning until fans demanded she face off against other boxers with famous fathers: George Foreman's daughter, Freeda Foreman, and Joe Frazier's daughter, Jacqui Frazier-Lyde. Though she was never able to set up a match against Freeda, Laila boxed against Jacqui and won, in the first-ever pay-per-view match between two women.

Laila claimed her first International Boxing Association world title in 2002. The next year, she beat Christy Martin, the woman who had inspired her to box, and the year after that, she defended her world title. Five years after picking up her father's sport, Laila had made it clear she was a name in her own right—but she still followed her dad's priceless advice: pretend there's a fly on the bag, and you have to hit it before it flies away. She spent hours hitting for speed, working on breathing techniques, mastering her balance, and finessing her footwork. She especially emphasized the importance of running to establish the lower body and core strength.

"I FELT LIKE I WAS FIGHTING FOR BOTH OF US."

When Laila retired in 2007, she had an undefeated record, with 24 victories and five world championships. Her father was a huge fan, though he was not able to attend many of her matches as his health declined due to Parkinson's Disease. He became her motivation, she told radio station WBUR.

AFTER THE RING

When she hung up her gloves, Laila turned her attention to building a lifestyle brand. A skilled home chef, she appeared as a contestant and host on multiple cooking shows—and even took a spin on *Dancing With the Stars!* She's launched beauty and hair care product lines as well as a line of spice blends and nutritional supplements. And she showed off her business skills on *The New Celebrity Apprentice*. If there is a consistent theme for Laila, it's that she never turns down a challenge.

Sabrina Ionescu

BE SCRAPPY

Eighteen minutes after Sabrina Ionescu was born, she got a little brother, a twin named Eddy. Growing up in California, the two were inseparable, even as they began to play sports, which they loved more than anything. Sabrina insisted on joining in every time Eddy and his friends picked up a basketball.

At first, it made no difference that Sabrina was a girl on a team full of boys, playing against another all-boys team. But eventually, Eddy and many of his friends got bigger and stronger. That was the case at home, too, when Sabrina and Eddy would play with their older brother, Andrei. The Ionescu boys never took it easy on their sister. "We fought and played games all the time, and I think that helped [my game]," Sabrina said.

Eddy was always her favorite hoops companion, and the twins would often play so late at night at a local park that their dad would have to shine his car headlights onto the court so they could see. Though she didn't know it at the time, Sabrina was developing the skills that would one day make her one of the best players in the college game. She was learning to be fast and scrappy and to use her brain when she couldn't rely on being physically stronger. "The guys were super competitive and didn't want a girl beating them," she says.

When Sabrina got to middle and high school and started playing on girls' teams, she had to adjust. But she quickly realized that all those years of scrambling and clawing for shots and rebounds had

paid off. She'd developed a varied skill set. She could shoot with insane accuracy, snare rebounds, and on top of that, she loved to pass, too. When Sabrina decided to go play at the University of Oregon for college, it was that all-around talent that sold the Ducks on her. They also got one of the most intense, hardest-working players in program history.

One of the toughest stats to achieve at any level of basketball is the triple-double. To earn one, a player has to rack up double digits in three statistical categories—usually points, rebounds, and assists. To make a habit out of tallying triple-doubles, a player must have sharp skills across the board, drive, and the selflessness to realize that sometimes a pass to an open teammate is better than trying to swish a ball through the net. Sabrina's early training primed her to be a triple-double machine. Still, few could have imagined when she got to campus just how many she'd achieve.

"I KNOW, JUST BY STARING AT THE BALL, WHO ON MY TEAM SHOT IT."

As a freshman, Sabrina ended her season with four. Impressive. As a sophomore, she added another six. Her junior year, then, she needed just two more triple-doubles to tie the NCAA record for women *and men*. She broke the record in the second month of the season, and she hasn't looked back. In 2020, she finished her senior year (which was shortened due to COVID), with eight more triple-doubles, bringing her to 26 for her career and more than doubling the previous record. She went on to be the first pick in the 2020 WNBA Draft, and though she was injured for most of her rookie season, she came back strong in 2021, recording her first professional triple-double in the third game of the year.

As Sabrina shattered records at Oregon, she also caught the eye of many elite male players. Kobe Bryant was a huge fan. Warriors guard Steph Curry described her as "a legend in her own right." It's been a long time since Sabrina played with the boys, but she's fine with breaking their records and turning them into some of her biggest fans.

Birgit Fischer

KEEP FIGHTING
TO THE VERY END

When Birgit Fischer's four-woman kayak streaked across the finish line at the 2004 Olympics in Athens, it was faster than any other boat in the water. Birgit, along with three teammates, took home the gold medal to cheers of support from fellow Germans. It was a thrilling day, but it was also a sight Birgit had become accustomed to.

That gold medal was the last of Birgit's career, which spanned more than two decades. In Athens, she also won a silver medal in the 500-meter race in a two-woman kayak. Birgit was no stranger to winning multiple medals at the same Olympics. What made 2004 special was Birgit's age. She was 42 years old, a star athlete on a boat with teammates decades younger than she was. (In the four-woman race, called K-4, the other Germans paddling with Birgit were 26, 26, and 19 years old.)

The gold medal Birgit won in Athens was the eighth of her Olympic career (she skipped the 1984 games because East Germany boycotted that year), making her the most-decorated German Olympian ever. With 12 total Olympic medals, she has the second-most of any woman to ever compete in the Summer Olympics. But the fact that tells the most about Birgit's career is this one: she's both the youngest and oldest Olympic kayaking champion, having won her first medal at just 18 years old, 24 years before her last.

Birgit won her first medal in 1980 in a K-1 race, meaning she was paddling solo in a kayak. Over her career, she was incredibly versatile, racing in one-woman, two-woman, and four-woman races, which were all 500 meters long. No matter how many other women competed in the same boat, Birgit's focus was the same, pulling her paddle through the choppy water with speed and fluidity and helping steer the boat straight ahead. Kayaking was her life, but she still managed to rack up a long list of accomplishments outside of the boat. At the start of her kayaking career, Birgit served in the army in East Germany. Later on, in the midst of her intense competition schedule, she also earned two degrees and raised two children.

"I see my success in competitive sport being down to my good timing and my clever training," Fischer said to Olympics.org. "I have looked after myself well and adapted my training again and again to my age, my stage of life, and my environment."

> **"NEVER FORGET YOUR LIFE OUTSIDE OF PADDLING."**

That adaptation has come as Birgit has repeatedly claimed she was about to retire. The first time she stated her intention to exit the sport was in 1988. Then she announced her retirement again after the 2000 Olympics. Each time, she came back better than ever. Though postponing retirement is not entirely unique, Birgit undertook something that very few elite athletes would attempt: for the last 12 years of her career, she trained without a coach. It was on her to design the workouts that would give her the upper body and core strength she needed to race so well in her kayak. She had no one to hold her accountable but herself, no coach to push her to work out on days when she didn't want to or when there was bad weather. She also had to handle all of her own scheduling and training calendars, relying only on herself to make sure she'd be in tip-top shape by the time of each event.

In 2000, Birgit was certain she was done. She'd ticked every box she wanted to tick in her career and had 10 Olympic medals already, in every type of competition kayak. But then in 2003, a documentary crew showed up at her home, asking her to get in a kayak for some footage. Back on the water, she couldn't resist daydreaming about competing again. "I wanted to challenge myself again," she told Olympics.org. "I wanted to know how and if my training plans could lead to success. I have always loved the great sense of freedom on the water, feeling nature directly below you, the combination of the water, the power, the dynamics, and the technology."

That's how Birgit ended up on the German Olympic team in 2004 for the K-4 (four-person) race. In Athens, the Germans felt threatened by a strong Hungarian team that thought it could take advantage of Birgit's retirement. But with Birgit back in the kayak, Germany had a chance, and it faced Hungary in the Olympic final. Hungary started strong, getting a good lead, but bit by bit, Birgit helped pull the Germans closer and closer. "In a split second, I think to myself that we might have started our final spurt too late," Birgit wrote in her autobiography about that race. "I try to convince myself that the second rank is also good. 'Why do I have those negative thoughts?', I think to myself. It was me who had always told the girls that nothing is lost until the very end. I feel my team wants to win and so do I!" That positive energy helped give Birgit and her teammates the jolt they needed, and they pulled even closer. Birgit felt exhausted, but she knew she had to keep pushing through the pain, no matter that her arms and legs felt ready to give up. Still, Birgit eyed the finish line. At 42, she wanted another gold medal—and she got it by less than a quarter of a second, edging the Hungarian team at the last moment and reminding herself that true champions keep fighting to the very end.

Tatyana McFadden

EMBRACE THE GIFTS YOU ARE GIVEN

When Tatyana McFadden was born in the Soviet Union in 1989, most of her family was living halfway around the world. She didn't know them yet: her two mothers, her grandmother, and the two girls who would become her younger sisters. All Tatyana knew was an orphanage in Leningrad (now called St. Petersburg), where her birth mother left her. Tatyana was born with spina bifida, a birth defect that caused her to be paralyzed from the waist down. The orphanage couldn't afford to buy Tatyana a wheelchair, so she pulled herself around with her hands and arms to keep up with the other kids. Most doctors expected Tatyana wouldn't live to see her teenage years.

But when Tatyana was six years old, a woman named Debbie McFadden walked into her orphanage, saw her, and couldn't get her out of her mind. Debbie worked for the U.S. government and had a special interest in children with disabilities. She adopted Tatyana, bringing her home to Baltimore. Debbie and her partner, Bridget O'Shaughnessy, later adopted two more girls, Hannah and Ruthi, both born in Albania. Hannah is missing the femur in her right leg. Ruthi has no physical disabilities—and she is the only one of the McFadden girls without any interest in becoming an athlete.

Tatyana got a wheelchair when Debbie brought her home. Her moms took her to an adaptive sports program and introduced her to as many sports as possible to build her strength. Within two years, she was racing in her chair, thanks in large part to the upper body strength she'd built in her early years at the orphanage. "That simple act of walking on my hands helped develop the muscles in my arms, back, and shoulders that have brought me so much success on the track and in life, convincing me that we are who we are from the moment we are born," Tatyana said in a speech at her graduation from the University of Illinois. "It is our job to take the gifts that we are given and use them the best way that we can."

In 2004, when she was 15, Tatyana competed in the Paralympics in Athens, Greece, against other athletes with disabilities. There, she won a silver medal in the 100-meter race and a bronze in the 200-meter race, competing in a sleek, low-to-the-ground chair with three wheels (one at the front and two larger wheels at the back). Racing chairs weigh about 20 pounds, and it's up to the racers to use their strength to power the chairs, which don't have gears to help control speed, like bikes do. Four years later, Tatyana came home from the Beijing Paralympics with three silver medals and one bronze, all in short-distance races. The longest event she participated in was the 800-meter race—though that was about to change.

In 2009, Tatyana decided to enter the Chicago Marathon. She was curious how it would go and had no experience with such a long race. She won, finishing so quickly that Debbie wasn't able to capture her crossing the finish line on camera. Suddenly, Tatyana was a marathoner too, and she's won races in New York, London, and Boston—some of the world's most prestigious marathons.

In 2012, Tatyana made history again, this time with Hannah by her side. At the Paralympics

> **"THE WORD 'CAN'T' IS NOT IN MY VOCABULARY."**

in London, the McFadden sisters both raced, and Tatyana won her first gold medals— three of them, in fact. She also took home a bronze medal. Hannah came in eighth in the 100-meter race. Four years later, both women competed in Rio de Janeiro, where Hannah came close to medaling, placing fourth in the 100 meter. Tatyana competed in the marathon, where she earned a silver medal, and she also took home another silver and four golds.

Over the years, Tatyana has devoted countless hours to training, doing everything from learning how to use her wheelchair to discovering speed to figuring out how to get in peak shape for long races. While training for marathons, she focuses on tempo work, alternating between fast movement and slower stretches. She's on the track for two to four hours each day. Like any other marathoner, she often logs about 100 miles each week, and she also makes time to visit the adaptive sports program where she first became enthralled with competition. Posters of her now hang on the walls there. In 2016, Tatyana wrote a book about her life for young readers called *Ya Sama!*, which is Russian for "I can do it!"—which pretty much says it all.

STRENGTH RUNS IN THE FAMILY

Debbie McFadden had a rare autoimmune disease, Guillain-Barré syndrome, which left her paralyzed from the neck down when she was in her twenties. She relied on an electric wheelchair for four years, and crutches for another eight years. Her experiences while disabled shaped her personally (leading her to adopt Tatyana and her sisters) and professionally. She became the U.S. commissioner of disabilities in 1989, under President George H. W. Bush. And she helped write the 1990 Americans with Disabilities Act.

When Tatyana was in high school, Debbie filed a lawsuit against their school district to enable Tatyana to race against participants in the same track events, rather than having to circle an empty track. They won the lawsuit and helped create the Maryland Fitness and Athletics Equity for Students with Disabilities Act, which requires schools to give disabled students equal opportunities to compete in sports.

WORLD CUP WINS ⦀⦀⦀ ⦀⦀⦀ ⦀⦀⦀
⦀⦀⦀ ⦀⦀⦀ ⦀⦀⦀ ⦀⦀⦀ ⦀⦀⦀ ⦀⦀⦀ ⦀⦀⦀
⦀⦀⦀ ⦀⦀⦀ ⦀⦀⦀ ⦀⦀⦀ ⦀⦀⦀
⦀⦀⦀ ⦀⦀

Lindsey Vonn

SET GOALS, BUT KNOW WHEN
ENOUGH IS ENOUGH

When Lindsey Kildow was a little girl growing up in the Minneapolis area, on Minnesota's flat Central Plains, there wasn't a mountain in sight—but there was plenty of snow. Still, Lindsey came from a skiing family. Her father and grandfather had both been competitive skiers, and on winter weekends, the family made trips to small, local slopes, like Buck Hill, where Lindsey was on skis by the time she was two. For longer family vacations, the Kildows made the 16-hour drive to Vail, Colorado.

Lindsey felt at home in the Rocky Mountains. A natural skier, she took alpine racing lessons and excelled to the point where her family made a decision: instead of commuting to Colorado each winter, Lindsey, her mother, and eventually her siblings would try living there permanently. At 12 years of age, Lindsey was just too good to not train full-time.

The move was a smart one. In 1999, when she was just 14 years old, Lindsey became the first American girl to win an elite race in Italy, called the Trofeo Topolino di Sci Alpino. The next year, she made her debut in a World Cup race, and by 2002, she'd qualified for her first Olympics, in Salt Lake City. Lindsey's star continued to rise, and she earned a silver medal in the Junior World Ski Championships in 2003, in the downhill division. At the same event the next year, she won a silver in downhill and a bronze in giant slalom. She earned the biggest medals yet of her career at the 2007 World Championships in Sweden (silver in downhill and super-G), and that year, she became Lindsey Vonn when she married a fellow skier, Thomas Vonn. (They divorced in 2013.) By the time she won gold in the downhill event at the 2010 Olympics (where she also won bronze in the super-G), Lindsey was considered the best woman skier in the world.

But her path was not without bumps. In late 2013, with the next Olympics set to kick off in Sochi, Russia in a matter of months, Lindsey tore a ligament in her knee while training. She hoped to push through, but as the Games got closer, that seemed impossible. In January 2014, she withdrew. "The reality has sunk in that my knee is just too unstable to compete at this level," she said. "I'm having surgery soon so that I can be ready for the World Championships at home in Vail next February."

> **"MY CHILDHOOD DREAM** WAS TO WIN THE OLYMPICS, AND I'VE DONE THAT. EVERYTHING ELSE IS ICING ON THE CAKE."

A week before the Olympics began, NBC announced that Lindsey would serve as a correspondent during the Games, informing viewers about skiing and about her own rehab. Viewers were thrilled to watch her, and Lindsey found a way to stay involved in spite of her injury.

Lindsey returned to competition a year after getting hurt, and she won a downhill race in Lake Louise, Alberta, Canada, in December 2014. Wearing red, white, and pink and tucked into a tight crouch, she flew down the hill in 1 minute, 50.48 seconds, taking her turns fast and aggressively enough to place first. It was just her second event since coming back from her injury, and she looked to be in great shape. Lindsey won a bronze medal at that season's World Championships in the super-G, and she kept racking up wins in World Cup events, hoping that one day she might beat the record held by Swedish skier Ingemar Stenmark, who won 86 World Cup races.

In 2016, Lindsey hit 70 World Cup wins. Though a broken arm kept her off her skis in 2017, she was healthy at the 2018 Olympics, where at 33 she became the oldest woman skier to medal when she took bronze in the downhill event. She was, as always, laser-focused on competing, refusing to let pain derail her goals. That perseverance set Lindsey apart. "My injuries made me stronger," she told reporters in Pyeongchang, South Korea. "When you're young, you ski and you win and you don't appreciate things. I've been in the fences so many times. I know so many doctors on a first-name basis that it's ridiculous."

Just six months after medaling, Lindsey announced her intention to retire after the 2018-19 season, still hoping to break the World Cup wins record. "Physically, I've gotten to the point where it doesn't make sense," Lindsey told NBC. "I really would like to be active when I'm older, so I have to look to the future and not just be so focused on what's in front of me."

The month after the Olympics, Lindsey logged her 82nd World Cup win. She continued training throughout that off-season, hoping to squeeze out five more victories. But early in her final season, Lindsey hurt her knee again while skiing in Colorado. When she returned, she wasn't 100%, and she considered retiring early, but she kept at it, flying to Sweden for the 2019 World Championships. In her last race, she won bronze in the downhill event, making her the oldest woman to ever medal in a World Championship event. Stenmark presented her with flowers afterwards.

"I was definitely the most nervous I've been in my entire life, and all I wanted to do was finish strong and have the ending that I've been dreaming of for my career," Lindsey said after the race. No matter that she was four victories short of her goal of 86 wins, Lindsey knew when it was time to quit, when her body had had enough.

Misty Copeland

IT'S NEVER TOO LATE
TO START

On June 30, 2015, the American Ballet Theater (ABT) announced its new principal dancer, which is a huge honor given to the best ballerina at the best ballet company in the United States. That day, the title went to Misty Copeland, a 32-year-old African American woman—and the first African American woman ever to be named a principal in ABT's long history.

Twenty years earlier, that outcome seemed impossible for Misty, who at 12 had never put on ballet slippers. Most ballet dancers begin classes when they're tiny, some still toddlers. But as a girl growing up in Southern California, Misty did most of her dancing to Mariah Carey's music. She never took ballet, even though she loved music and movement. Instead, she participated in her middle school's drill team and admired Nadia Comăneci, the former Olympic gymnast (see page 60). It wasn't until Misty was 13 that she took her first ballet class—about a decade later than many of the other girls she began to dance with. The instructor at the local Boys & Girls Club was impressed with Misty's natural ability right away. That's not how Misty remembers it, though. She was embarrassed and felt like she was far behind the other dancers, unable to follow instructions correctly because she was unsure of the terminology.

When Misty was 15, she competed to win the Los Angeles Music Center Spotlight Award for ballet. She chose to perform a

> ## "KNOWING THAT IT'S NEVER BEEN DONE BEFORE I THINK **MAKES ME FIGHT** EVEN HARDER."

complicated piece from *Don Quixote* for the panel of intimidating judges. The choreography called for a big finish—32 difficult turns called fouettés in a row. She practiced six days a week for a month, often followed by a television crew documenting her journey. She had always been able to pull off the tough choreography. But as the performance loomed, she began to falter on her final turns. For the first time, she was truly nervous. At the last minute, she and her teacher rechoreographed the end of the number in a parking garage, with Misty dancing in her sneakers. Then, she got on stage, nailed the new ending (with 16 fouettés instead of 32), and won the prize! And she learned the importance of always having a backup plan!

Misty joined ABT in 2000, when she was 18, and immediately, she injured her back. Forced to wear a brace, she wasn't able to dance for a year, and as she eased back into ballet, she found her body had changed, becoming curvier than the average ballerina's. Still, Misty pressed on, working her way up through the company's ranks. In 2007, she became a soloist. Misty was 24 when she was promoted, making her one of the youngest dancers to ever win a soloist role at ABT. It had long ago stopped mattering that she hadn't spent her entire childhood in tutus. Her talent and hard work were all that mattered as Misty developed into a ballerina known for her athletic style as well as her ability to display emotion through the subtlest movements.

Five days a week, Misty trains and rehearses for about nine hours, learning and refining choreography and dances, repeating pirouette after plié after arabesque. She's stressed the importance of healthy eating to power her through those challenging days, and she starts every morning with a long series of calf raises to wake her legs for the exercise ahead. Misty also focuses on mindfulness and posture, keeping her brain alert and her body limber. She stretches as much as possible, throughout her day and not just before and after physical activity. "I think it's important for people to see beyond this picture-perfect effortless thing that you put onstage," Misty told *Glamour*. "We're doing what football players are doing and basketball players are doing behind the scenes."

As Misty's career progressed, she found even more visibility. For much of her time at ABT, she was the only African American woman in the company, earning comparisons to Jackie Robinson, the Black player who crossed the color barrier in Major League Baseball. Like Jackie, Misty stood out, and she used her talent to earn opportunities outside of traditional ballet. She starred in a Diet Dr. Pepper commercial, toured with Prince, and eventually earned an Under Armour endorsement. Her ad campaign showed the world how athletic and demanding ballet is. Later, Misty designed her own line of athleticwear for Under Armour. Now ballerinas and athletes everywhere can sport outfits designed by the best dancer of her generation, who first put on pointe shoes late—but not too late to catch up.

Brooke Raboutou

KEEP YOUR HEAD IN THE GAME

Brooke Raboutou was born to climb. Her father, Didier Raboutou, was one of the top French rock climbers in the 1980s and 1990s, winning several World Cup titles, and her mother, an American rock climber named Robyn Erbesfield-Raboutou, earned four consecutive World Cup titles in the 1990s. While Didier installed climbing walls in his children's playroom, their mother, Robyn, founded a kid's climbing gym in their hometown of Boulder, Colorado. Brooke has an older brother, Shawn, who is also an elite rock climber.

Thanks to her parents' enthusiasm—and probably her genetics, too—Brooke started dabbling in climbing as soon as she could walk. She was accompanying her parents on exciting outdoor climbs by the time she was four years old. At seven, she began competing, with technique that exceeded the skills of much older climbers. After all, Brooke spent so much time at her mother's climbing facility that by the time she started competing, scaling towering indoor rock walls felt almost like second nature. Summers spent climbing in France also made her fall even more in love with the sport, as she was able to get outdoors rather than spend most of her time in indoor facilities.

When Brooke was just 11 years old, she completed a climb that would make most adults shudder. In traditional climbing, athletes ascend rock faces without the help of gear (though they do have gear with them in case of emergency), relying simply on their hands and feet. Such climbs have grades, from 5.1 to 5.15d, depending on their difficulty (though the scale keeps expanding as climbers find tougher routes). A grade of 5.1 is easy, and those numbers ascend all the way to 5.15d, the hardest for now. In fact, there is only one route in the world that has a 5.15d grade. But there are plenty of 5.14b climbs, and at 11, Brooke became the youngest person in the world to conquer such a tough route. Her climb took place in Rodellar, Spain, and the most difficult stretch came at the end, when the rock offered only small holds, which were far apart. Since Brooke wasn't as tall as other climbers, and her arms and legs weren't nearly as long, she had to struggle to stretch from one hold to the next. But by climbing carefully and precisely, she made it to the end. "It was beautiful to watch and the entire valley of Rodellar was cheering for her," Brooke's mother told Climbing.com.

> **"WHEN I'M ON A HIGH ROCK, I FEEL I'M IN CONTROL AND JUST HAPPY."**

Brooke has completed many of the world's most difficult climbs since then, including a 5.14c in Kentucky when she was 13. But there are multiple disciplines to what she does, beyond just climbing to great heights, and Brooke has also impressed fans with her achievements in bouldering. In that kind of climbing, Brooke has no safety gear, just her hands, feet, and shoes, as she climbs rock faces that are much lower to the ground than the ones in traditional climbing. That versatility helped Brooke in a big way when the International Olympic Committee announced both that climbing would debut at the 2020 Olympics in Tokyo (which were subsequently postponed to 2021) and that the competition would have three parts. Each competitor will compete in bouldering, speed climbing (where two climbers race, climbing identical routes), and lead climbing (where climbers, using safety ropes, try to climb as high as possible in a set amount of time). Brooke excels in all three areas, while many older climbers admitted they'd done very little speed climbing before they learned about the Olympic format.

Though Brooke has an incredibly physically demanding training regimen, she also knows that success in climbing hinges on mental preparation. She likes to visualize her routes before she takes off, imagining where her hands and feet will go, how she'll best grip, and what exact route she'll need to take. She has been known to meditate and use breath work to help her concentration, and she's tried yoga, too. "Without believing, it's hard to focus and nearly impossible to perform to your capability," Brooke wrote on Instagram in 2019. "There wasn't a single World Cup this year where I was close to satisfied with my performance. With the help of my beloved parents, I realized that it wasn't my physical strength that was lacking, but my mind that was elsewhere. Listening to their wisdom from their many years of high level competition, I am learning how much power the mind has over performance."

Despite so many years spent climbing around the world, Brooke knows she can never lose focus. Just two months after she qualified for the Olympics, she was reminded why. Climbing at a competition in Albuquerque, she reached the third problem (that's the term for a specific route, and in bouldering competitions, climbers complete several before they're finished). She took what she called a "bad" fall, hurting her knee enough that she sat out the rest of the event. She was back in the gym soon after, but the fall helped Brooke to refocus and stay alert in preparation for her biggest competition yet.

Gabby Douglas

DON'T LET YOUR DOUBTS WIN

In 2012, just a few months before she was scheduled to compete for a spot on the United States Olympic team—a spot most expected her to win—Gabby Douglas told her mother that she wanted to quit the sport. She had a new path in mind: she'd run track and work at Chick-Fil-A.

At the time, Gabby was 16 and wildly homesick. Two years earlier, she'd moved across the country, from her home in Virginia to the cornfields of Iowa, to enroll in a better training program. Since Gabby was little, she'd displayed all the signs of gymnastics potential, with high energy and an adventurous spirit. "I was always an adrenaline junkie," she told *TIME* magazine. "When I was three, I would climb up the door frames on walls and just sit there. From a young age, I did it for fun. I never knew it was going to be something that I did— my career. I just fell in love with gymnastics." Gabby was built for the sport, but she had plenty of obstacles to overcome before she reached its highest level.

For one, Gabby's family was homeless during the first year of her life, living out of the back of a van and doing whatever they could to scrape by. With four children—Gabby was the youngest— her parents had many mouths to feed. Her mother somehow managed to enroll the baby of the family in gymnastics when she was six years old. By then, her father had left his wife and kids behind.

Gabby could pull off a full-twisting double backflip by age 12 and was stellar on the uneven bars. But she was also bullied at times at the gym because of her skin color. She never felt like she fit in, and when she got an opportunity to head to Iowa, which seemed like a world away, change was appealing. Maybe, she thought, she'd be more accepted there. Gabby was 14 when she arrived in the Midwest in 2010, and her career began to flourish. She competed in her first international competition the next year, and as the youngest performer at the 2011 World Championships, helped her team win gold.

> **"YOU HAVE TO BELIEVE THAT YOU ARE GOOD ENOUGH, AND YOU HAVE TO NOT GIVE UP."**

But before the London Olympics in 2012, her first, Gabby didn't feel like a winner. She missed being home with everyone she loved. In fact, during her two years in Iowa, Gabby saw her mother only four times. It was on one of those visits that she said she wanted to return home and give up the sport in which she seemed poised to be a star. Her mother knew that wasn't what her daughter really wanted—it was just a product of homesickness—and she turned to one of the signature pep talks she's given Gabby over the years. On her website, Gabby recalls what her mother told her that day in Iowa: "Life is not easy. You have to fight and just refuse to quit."

That's exactly what Gabby did, refocusing on her dreams and channeling her attention from loneliness to competition. In London, she won the all-around gold medal as well as the team gold and became a fan favorite, wowing crowds with her strength, fearlessness, and versatility. Going into the floor exercise, which was the final component of the all-around competition, Gabby led the field of 24 gymnasts. But she was competing against the world's top talent, and she knew there was no room for error. She started, and the crowd showed their support. Fans clapped along to her music.

Gabby rode that positive energy through the entire routine, springing high into the air and sticking her landings nearly perfectly. When the final floor exercise score came in and Gabby was still on top, she made history, becoming the first African American woman to win gold in the all-around gymnastics competition.

"I was so honored to go to the Olympics and compete and even be the first African American to win the individual all-around," Gabby told ESPN. "I wanted to quit, but I'm so glad that everyone around me supporting me told me to stick with the sport and that you can do it."

It was impossible for Gabby to forget her mother's pep talk or the tough love her family gave her when they thought she might quit. (In fact, they told her if she was going to leave the sport, they were going to drive her to her Iowa host family's house, and she'd have to tell them face-to-face that she was giving up.) Near or far, Gabby's family's crucial encouragement helped her cope with everything from success to social media critique, and she's not shy about asking for advice now that she's gotten older.

That support helped convince Gabby to keep competing after London, even though she'd be 20 by the time of the next Olympics. In gymnastics, that's old. But Gabby knew she had a chance, so she took some time off from the sport to recharge and then dove back in 2015. The time away helped Gabby detox from the stress of 2012, and when she returned, she was three inches taller, standing 5'2.5". She used that height to her advantage, adjusting on the bars quickly and feeling thankful for her added strength. The U.S. coach was impressed with what she saw, awarding Gabby a spot on the team that traveled to Rio de Janeiro in 2016. In the leadup to those Olympics, she told ESPN, "Before, I would think to myself, 'I *think* I have this.' Now I am more competitive and aggressive. I think, 'Yes. I have this. Let's go.'"

And just like that, she helped the team win another gold medal.

Michelle Kwan

STAY POSITIVE, AND CELEBRATE SECOND PLACE, TOO

When Michelle Kwan retired from figure skating in 2006, she was 25 years old and the most decorated American athlete in her sport. She'd competed in two Olympics, winning a silver medal in 1998 and a bronze in 2002. Between 1996 and 2003, she'd won five World Championships, and she was the top U.S. competitor in 1996 and then again for eight years in a row starting in 1998. She was as memorable as she was marketable: for much of Michelle's career, she earned more money than any other figure skater in the United States, male or female, from prizes and endorsement contracts. She was a role model and a household name, famous for her elegant performances on the ice and her positive attitude off of it.

Michelle's path to figure skating greatness began when she was five. Her older siblings skated, and she began to tag along, falling in love with the sport. When Michelle was eight, she began to seriously train with her sister Karen. The two sisters practiced for more than three hours per day, setting alarms for 4:30 a.m. so they could get to the rink before school, and they'd return once classes were finished. Figure skating is an expensive hobby, and when it became too much for her parents' bank accounts, the community pitched in to help Michelle stay on the ice. Everyone knew she was too talented to quit. "My parents didn't have the means to provide brand-new skates, flashy costumes, or ice time," Michelle told *The Cut* in 2017.

"THE GRIT AND PERSEVERANCE THAT YOU LEARN IN SPORTS—THAT IS **A LIFE LESSON.**"

"They were barely juggling multiple jobs, providing a roof over our heads, feeding us, working at the restaurant, my dad was working at a phone company, and then they gave me this crazy opportunity to ice skate!"

When Michelle went to her first national championships in skating, she did so wearing borrowed costumes and secondhand skates that had another girl's name written on them. They skates were slightly too big, but Michelle's dad crossed out the other name and wrote his daughter's, and they were good enough. "I didn't feel disadvantaged," she told *The Cut*. "I felt empowered because I had these opportunities. I was going to try to make the most of it."

By the time Michelle began to skate on a bigger stage, she was known for her remarkable consistency. She might not have achieved the highest heights on her jumps or the fastest speeds, but she rarely made an error. She skated quietly, earning admirers for her graceful movements, especially her spirals, where she glided on one foot while raising the other foot above hip level, similar to an arabesque in ballet. Michelle's spirals were the strongest element of her skating, and she was applauded for length she achieved, how well she transitioned in and out of them, and her speed. She was also one of very few figure skaters who could spin in both directions. As she got older, Michelle learned to be more expressive and faster, and her technique edged even closer to perfection.

Before the 1998 Olympics in Nagano, Japan, Michelle hurt her foot. She pressed pause on training for a while and then won a national championship despite having an injured toe. At the Olympics, she prepared for her short program, which has required elements and lasts 2 minutes, 40 seconds, and for the more flexible free skate, which both determine who will medal. Michelle was a heavy favorite along with fellow American Tara Lipinski, and though she was in the lead after the short program, Michelle won silver after Tara topped her in the free skate. "It might not be the color medal I wanted, but I'll take it," Michelle said.

Michelle continued training for another four years, preparing for the 2002 Olympics. There, she again contended after the short program. But in the free skate, she fell on her triple flip, and ended up winning the bronze. She handled her disappointment with grace and remained upbeat about the fact that she'd won a medal in the first place. "It's not so bad getting silver and bronze and winning five world titles," she said. "There's just one thing that's missing in the repertoire. When I look back, I wouldn't have changed anything. I couldn't have worked harder. There was the dedication to the sport. The amazing family and team that I had. The mindset, the drive, the motivation, the grit, it was all there."

When Michelle withdrew from the 2006 Olympics after suffering an injury, she did so in tears. She'd been hurt off and on for a while but had held onto hope that she'd be able to compete in one more Olympics. But she was just in too much pain. When she recovered, she focused on her education, and though Michelle retired without a gold medal, she still made it to the top of her sport.

When her skating career ended, Michelle did not disappear from public life. Instead, she applied her determination and experience with world travel to her next career in international relations. She became a public envoy for Secretary of State Condoleezza Rice, talking to students around the world about educational and cultural issues. Later, she worked as a staffer for Hillary Clinton during her presidential campaign and assisted with Joseph Biden's 2020 campaign and in planning his 2021 inauguration. A generation of fans will always remember Michelle's generous words, her positive attitude, and her extraordinary talent.

Julie Krone

GET **BACK** ON THE HORSE

On June 5, 1993, Julie Krone became the first woman jockey to win a Triple Crown race, at the Belmont Stakes. The Belmont is one of the three races—along with Kentucky Derby and the Preakness Stakes—that make up the Triple Crown, the most prestigious events in horse racing. Astride Colonial Affair, a three-year-old thoroughbred with a dark brown coat and long odds to win, Julie took first at the race in Belmont, New York. With the surprise win, which the *Los Angeles Times* called "a perfect race," Julie made history. Then she burst into happy tears.

Horse racing was at the time (and still is) a male-dominated sport, and before Julie's win, critics wondered whether women had the strength to maneuver horses that weighed more than 1,000 pounds at the high speeds necessary to win. Julie proved they could, using every bit of her 4'10", 100-pound frame to clutch the reins and steer a massive horse around muddy tracks, dodging 12 other animals running nearly as fast and just as hard. Then, a decade after her Belmont victory, she became the first woman to win a Breeders' Cup title, too, riding a horse named Halfbridled. But what happened between those two big wins might provide the most important lesson of her career.

In August 1993, Julie was thrown from her horse while racing at the Saratoga Race Course in New York, breaking her right ankle, injuring her elbow, and suffering a bruise to her heart muscle. She nearly died! Her life may have been saved by the two-pound safety vest she chose to wear that day, trading a tiny bit of added weight for some insurance against injury. After having surgery and rehabilitating, Julie returned to racing, anything but scared away by the injury.

Then, not even two weeks after her first race back, Julie was hurt again. This time, she broke both of her hands at a race in Florida when she was thrown to the track by her horse, who was also injured. Physically, she recovered. But in her head, Julie became more uncertain while riding.

In horse racing, jockeys play an important factor. A great jockey can't make a slow horse fast, but a jockey with tons of talent can get a strong horse to pull ahead of the pack through smart steering, keen vision, and brainpower. Jockeys need to have the confidence to steer their horses through narrow gaps that are often a dangerous squeeze—but which are necessary to winning races. After the accident, Julie found herself circling other horses, taking longer routes to pass, which made it tougher to move up the standings. In 1999, she decided to retire. By then, she'd racked up 3,545 victories and her mounts' "purse earnings" totaled $81 million. Purse earnings are the amount of money up for grabs in a race. The bulk goes to the owners of the top three or four winning horses, with the jockeys

"YOU DON'T FEEL AFRAID ON THE TRACK. YOU DON'T FEEL ANYTHING. ALL THAT STUFF ABOUT THE WIND IN YOUR FACE AND THE FEAR AND THE THRILL—FORGET IT. YOU'RE TOO BUSY RUNNING THE RACE."

receiving 10% of the owner's share. Jockeys are also paid a fee to ride, whether or not they win.

The next year, Julie was inducted into the National Museum of Racing and Hall of Fame, the first woman to earn that honor. She transitioned into television almost immediately after retiring, using her knowledge to bring color and smart analysis to broadcasted races. At the end of 2002, though, Julie got an itch. Sitting in a TV booth and conducting interviews just wasn't enough for an adrenaline-seeker, so she decided to come out of retirement. "I had to prove to myself that I could face my fears and be back at the top level of competition," Julie told *USA Today* of her decision to return to the track.

And quickly, she was back at the top of the game. Ten years after her astonishing win at the Belmont Stakes and four years after her decision to retire, Julie raced to victory at the Breeders' Cup and won 11 other major races that season. But at the end of 2003, another injury, this time to her ribs, derailed Julie, and though she got back on her horse briefly after recovering, she decided it was finally time to end her career for good not long after. With 3,704 wins, Julie still has the most wins by any woman in the history of horse racing, and her success and fame have inspired the next generation. Julie told ESPN in 2001, "I approached the sport like there wasn't a gender issue, and I wouldn't participate in the mindset of 'she is just a girl.'"

A NATURAL ON HORSEBACK

Julie grew up on a horse farm in western Michigan, right off the coast of Lake Michigan. She fell in love with horses thanks to her mother, Judi, who had ridden as an equestrian as a young woman. "When Julie was 2," Judi told the *New York Times*, "I had her on a pony, and I was leading him around the farm with just a lead rope on, no bridle. I dropped the rope for a moment and he really took off, bucking like crazy, but her little butt never left his back—and she was laughing." At age five, Julie won a competition at the local county fair in the under-18 division, competing against children more than 10 years older than she was. Though she was clearly a gifted equestrian, after watching 18-year-old jockey Steve Cauthen win a Triple Crown race, Julie decided that *that* was for her.

Sabre Norris

COMPETE WITH **HEART**

When Sabre Norris was 11 years old, she became the youngest surfer to ever earn a wild-card entry at a major Australian surfing event, the 2016 Sydney International Women's Pro. There, before even paddling out to meet her first wave, the tween became a sensation, doing television interviews about how exciting it was to be invited to such a prestigious competition. She charmed viewers across the continent. Speaking on Australia's *Today Show*, Sabre pointed out that she'd get a great reward no matter how she placed, because even the last-place finisher would win $250—which Sabre joked that she'd spend on donuts. She finished 25th out of 94 competitors, a long way from last.

Sabre's story went viral in the surfing world, but she'd become plenty famous years earlier for her Internet personality and skateboarding skills. At just nine years old, Sabre had mastered a 540 trick, where she'd catch air on her skateboard and spin 540 degrees—a full rotation and a half—before landing. In the video from the day Sabre finally pulled off the trick, she can be seen trying over and over, coming out of the spin at the top of the halfpipe but never quite landing properly. Each time, she falls as she skates back down the ramp. Sometimes, she yells with frustration as she skids along the bottom of the halfpipe on her kneepads. Other times, she barely pauses before picking up her board to go again. But on her 75th try, Sabre finally lands the trick, known as a "McTwist," which is one of the most difficult in skateboarding. She shrieks with joy. "I can't believe it!" she pants into the camera, a huge grin on her face.

Sabre is still known for her screams, her laughs, and her silly attitude. She and her siblings—Biggy, Sockie, Naz, Disco, and Charm—are famous on YouTube for posting funny and inspirational videos of their lives and their athletic achievements. (Sockie, Naz, and Disco also love skateboarding and surfing and hope to follow in Sabre's footsteps.) Sabre's personality is so infectious that every time she does a television interview, she seems to make friends with the newscaster, entertaining viewers with goofy stories about her family. Before the Sydney International Women's Pro, she talked for a long time about her efforts to eat healthy meals and how that helped her dad, (a former Olympic swimmer who beat American star Michael Phelps to win a bronze medal in the Sydney Olympics), lose weight. Sabre joked about how much ice cream her dad used to eat, telling the audience how he'd have to suck in his stomach for photos. The clip went viral.

> ## "DON'T GET ANGRY, OR THE RAIL WILL GET YOU."

Sabre has been invited multiple times to appear on *The Ellen Show* in the United States, talking about her love of buffet meals and bursting with happiness at getting to meet Ellen DeGeneres, the show's host. Dressed in a sparkly headband and pink tulle skirt on her first visit to the show, Sabre jumped with joy, full of energy and excitement. She explained how her dad had wanted her to become a swimmer, but she had no interest. "If I want to be a swimmer, I don't have to do any chores, but if I want to be a surfer, I've got to do this gnarly list of jobs," Sabre told Ellen, laughing. She always finishes her chores, she explained, so that she can spend as much time riding the waves or at the skate park as possible.

But it hasn't been all riding waves and landing McTwists. In 2018, Sabre learned that she had a serious medical problem, called a Chiari malformation. Because of it, she hasn't grown as much as most 15-year-olds, and the fact that she was so small (4'5" and 84 lbs) became a concern. In 2019, Sabre began taking growth hormones, and she shared details of her condition on her Instagram with her usual positive attitude. Sabre hasn't let her diagnosis get in the way of her goal to compete in the Olympics in skateboarding, either. In 2018, the year she was diagnosed, Sabre won a silver medal at the X Games, completing another McTwist and becoming one of just three women to pull off the trick successfully there. After the competition, she looked poised to earn an Olympic spot, and she's still hoping to. "The medical result means I need to show more heart and put in more hours than anyone else," she said. "If you've got something wrong with you, you've got to accept it and not hide it. You need to tell someone about it, so you don't feel so alone." Between her family of eight and her millions of fans, Sabre is definitely not alone.

THE NORRIS NUTS

Though Sabre is the most famous active athlete in the Norris family, all of her siblings share in her Internet fame—including Charm, a baby girl born in December 2019 who had more than 180,000 Instagram followers by the time she was two weeks old. That's because Charm's siblings are such hits on all forms of social media, especially YouTube, where their page "The Norris Nuts," has millions of subscribers. On the channel, Sabre and her siblings entertain fans in lots of crazy ways. They have competed to see who could eat the most pizza or burgers, or who would leave a bed, bathroom, or swimming pool last. They even posted a suspenseful video where they debated (and then decided on) Charm's name. At the end, Charm yawns and spits up.

Ginny Capicchioni

CREATE YOUR **OWN** OPPORTUNITIES

At Sacred Heart University in Fairfield, Connecticut, Ginny Capicchioni was a superstar lacrosse goalie, setting records constantly over the course of her career, from 1998 to 2001. Despite standing just 5'4" and having plenty of net to protect, Ginny's numbers for saves in a season, career saves, single-season save percentage, and career save percentage were *all* the best in Sacred Heart history. She also won 32 games over the course of her college career—yet another Sacred Heart record.

Ginny played field hockey in college, too, and though one sport was played with a more traditional stick, the other with a pole with a net on the end, the two complemented each other, helping her become a standout in each. But lacrosse was where Ginny made her name and where she saw her future—in part because a future in professional lacrosse seemed possible, if still a long shot.

In the United States in the early 2000s, there weren't many opportunities for women to play pro lacrosse. Still, Ginny wanted her shot, and she had an idea. In 2001, Jen Adams, an attacker (in lacrosse, that's an offensive player who scores most of the goals), was drafted into the National Lacrosse League, a U.S. men's league. Jen was the first woman to earn that honor, but she didn't make it past exhibition games on the roster of the Washington Power. When it came time for Ginny to try to crack into the league, she took a different approach,

> ## "THERE'S A BIG DIFFERENCE BETWEEN BEING A PLAYER AND BEING A PRESENCE. **BE A PRESENCE.**"

attending open tryouts across the country and standing tough in goal as men winged shots at her. The New Jersey Storm's coaches were impressed enough to sign her to a contract a year after Jen was drafted. Ginny had taken a risk, and she'd found her opportunity.

When Ginny joined the Storm, she couldn't have known what to expect. One woman had played through preseason exhibitions, but if Ginny were to make the regular-season roster, it would be uncharted territory. The Storm needed a third-string goalie, someone who was tough enough to hang in the net at every practice but who was selfless enough to know he (or she) might not get to see any game action. Ginny got the job, and when she was included on the Storm's opening day roster in 2003, she made history. She soon earned minutes in a game, too, becoming the first woman in North America to play in a professional men's lacrosse game. Some people were thrilled at the news. Others were horrified.

Critics talked about Ginny's shorter stature, how she'd never be able to cover the lacrosse net, which in the men's game is six feet high by six feet wide. Most men in goal were close to a foot taller than she was, and on top of that, she'd struggled in scrimmages, making fans worry about what would happen in games. And though the coach of the Storm spoke highly of Ginny and said she'd beaten out several men for the spot, he also admitted she wouldn't play

SHINING THE SPOTLIGHT ON GOALIES

In addition to honing her talent on the field, Ginny founded a company called Gladiator Lacrosse that trains male and female goaltenders. Her company also created a player-rating index for lacrosse goalies called Goal Guardian. By measuring skill sets and athletic ability, the system is designed to help NCAA coaches—who otherwise don't have a lot to go on in determining the best fit for their teams—recruit goalies.

unless several players wound up hurt. But in April of that year, Ginny found herself suited up, ready to show men what a woman could do in the net. Though it wasn't a particularly memorable outing, Ginny's debut spoke volumes to women hoping for careers in lacrosse.

After her year with the team in New Jersey, Ginny decided to take her 40 pounds of goalie gear and head north to Canada, where she played in the Canadian Lacrosse Association for nine years with men and women. With her massive pads taking over her tiny frame, she played across the league and was never afraid to head to a new city or tackle a new opportunity. She was also named to the USA World Team, competing in the World Indoor Lacrosse Championships alongside a team full of men. (She had to share a locker room with her teammates, changing at different times.) At the 2011 World Indoor Lacrosse Championships in Prague, Ginny saved 93% of shots taken against her in goal. "I expect to keep the ball out of the net and beyond that, I don't care what anybody thinks," Ginny told ThePostGame.com before the game in Prague. "I'm sure they have lives and great personalities, and the ones I've met are really nice. When it comes to playing on a men's team, if you get your job done, they don't mind that you're there."

It's impossible to say how Ginny's mindset about lacrosse would have been different had she never played with men. But it's clear that she took away from that time a thirst for knowledge and coaching—anything that could help give her an edge over players who were almost always bigger and stronger than she was. She's been working to share what she learned ever since she retired in 2016, after a long and successful career in the net. In addition to running her company, Ginny has coached at colleges across the United States, including the University of Pennsylvania, the University of Michigan, and the University of Louisville, helping the next generation of women prepare for the grueling, physical game of lacrosse!

Jackie Joyner-Kersee

NEVER **FORGET** YOUR ROOTS

When Jackie Joyner-Kersee was a teenager in the 1970s, she competed in track and field, basketball, and volleyball for East St. Louis Lincoln Senior High School. She realized she and her teammates weren't always treated the same as students from other, less diverse schools when they traveled for meets and games. Born and raised in East St. Louis, a crime-ridden neighborhood across the Mississippi River from downtown St. Louis, Jackie learned young that her roots raised eyebrows. As a Black teenager traveling to compete, she sometimes felt there were places she wasn't welcome. Once, a scorekeeper decided not to record her time in a race. Still, Jackie earned big-time honors in high school, winning the National Junior Pentathlon championship each year.

Jackie's talent took her out of East St. Louis after high school: to the 1980 Olympic trials and to University of California, Los Angeles (UCLA) for college. Though busy competing for one of the top universities in the country, Jackie was homesick in Los Angeles, calling home as often as she could. When her mother passed away during her freshman year, Jackie missed home, her family, and her community.

At UCLA, Jackie ran track and played basketball, scoring 1,167 points over four seasons on the court. She took a break from hoops in 1983-84, though, for another commitment: she needed to devote most of her time to training for Olympic track and field. In 1984, she won her first Olympic medal, a silver in the heptathlon, which is one

of the most challenging and complicated events in the sport. It's really seven events: the 100-meter hurdles, high jump, shot put, 200-meter sprint, long jump, javelin throw and, finally, the 800-meter race. To master such a wide variety of skills took tremendous dedication, and Jackie went on to compete in four Olympic Games from 1984 to 1996, winning six medals: three gold, a silver, and two bronze. Three came in the heptathlon, another three in the long jump.

By the time Jackie retired, she was widely regarded as the best woman ever to compete in track and field. She was inducted into the USA Track and Field Hall of Fame in 2004, and she could have taken her career in dozens of directions. She chose to devote herself to the philanthropic work she'd begun while still competing. "Growing up in East St. Louis . . . [I wanted] to do whatever I could to make my parents proud by working hard and staying committed to whatever goal I had set for myself," Jackie told PBS in 2010. She had gotten her start thanks to sports programming at a community center, and she wanted to ensure that girls and boys in East St. Louis might have the same opportunities. In 1988, she founded the Jackie Joyner-Kersee Foundation, and nine years later, she began work on creating a community center in her hometown.

In 2007, she helped found Athletes for Hope, which educates professional athletes about philanthropy and charitable causes. Nearly 20 years after she finished competing, Jackie is working to help more young athletes rise to the top of their game.

> **"I HOPE TO LIVE FOREVER, BUT I KNOW I WON'T. THE CENTER WILL ALWAYS BE THERE AND WILL CONTINUE TO HAVE AN IMPACT."**

Marlen Esparza

CONVINCE YOURSELF YOU'RE UNBEATABLE

When Marlen Esparza was 11 years old, she showed up at Houston's Elite Boxing gym looking for lessons. She was short and skinny with long hair—she didn't look the part of a boxer in any way—and the coach was not impressed. Besides, he told Marlen, he didn't train girls. Marlen didn't listen.

She hung around the gym and earned admiration for her tenacity. Once she got a chance to compete, she was hooked, even if there weren't clear opportunities for women in the ring. Over the next decade, as she continued to compete, the sport evolved dramatically. In 2012, when Marlen was 22, the International Olympic Committee (IOC) approved women's boxing. Marlen was finally going to get her big chance! At that point, she had a career record of 69-2 and had ranked first in her weight class, flyweight (106–112 pounds), since she was 16. At the London Olympics, she made it all the way to the semifinal round before losing to Ren Cancan of China, a three-time world champion. Still, she brought home a bronze, and to her great surprise, the people of Houston were proud of her. The city fell in love with the woman who had become a role model to feisty little girls. "When I was younger, I didn't have the privilege of someone doing it before me, so I didn't have anyone to ask, 'how do I do this?' or 'what's the next move?'" Marlen told *Houstonia* magazine.

The example she sets is one of extreme focus. At most boxing events, the competitors stay together in the same hotel. But as part of her mental preparation, Marlen stays elsewhere, on her own dime, as she works to convince herself that she's superior to her opponents— that she can't be beat. That mental training goes along with grueling physical workouts to refine her speed and agility. She needs these advantages as she's usually smaller than her opponents.

Marlen followed her Olympic bronze with a gold medal at the International Boxing Association world championships in 2014 and a bronze at the same event in 2016. These high-profile wins caught the attention of Oscar De La Hoya, a former world champion boxer who started a promotion company. Golden Boy Promotions signed Marlen, their first female client. And then they got to work producing major events where she could fight. Instead of just collecting medals, Marlen could now earn money for her fights, and her first pro event drew huge excitement. Wearing all red, with a Nike swoosh buzzed into the side of her head, Marlen stood in the corner of the ring, eyes narrowed. When the fight began, she delivered her punches with precision, head down and fists flying. She pushed her opponent up against the ropes and dominated for the entire fight. She won in four rounds. The event was televised on ESPN, so the world could see Marlen break into a wide smile when she won. Before the fight, she'd told ESPN, "I was born for this," and that night, the crowd agreed.

In her first five fights, she was undefeated. In 2018, she got married and became pregnant, forcing her to step out of the ring. Her son was born in January 2019, and she returned to the ring that April, ready to go.

> **"I AM A MOM, I AM NURTURING, AND I'M TRYING TO RAISE A HUMAN BEING, BUT AT THE SAME TIME, I HAVE TO HAVE MY GAME FACE ON."**

Amy Van Dyken-Rouen

FIND A WAY **AROUND** THE WALL

When Amy Van Dyken-Rouen was a 19-year-old swimmer competing for the University of Arizona, she missed her chance to make her first Olympic team, placing fourth at the Olympic trials in 1992 in the 50-meter freestyle. It was a disappointing finish for the teenager in a sport where it's rare for athletes to make their first Olympics once they've graduated from college—and Amy would be 23 by the time of the next Games.

That didn't worry her, though, and she came back stronger in 1996—so strong, in fact, that she became the first American woman to win four gold medals at a single Olympics. (She placed first in the 50-meter freestyle, the 100-meter butterfly, the 4x100-meter freestyle relay, and the 4x100-meter medley relay.) In the years after 1996, Amy battled shoulder injuries and had to undergo several surgeries, taking two years off from serious training. Still, she qualified for the 2000 Olympics in Sydney, where she added two more gold medals to her collection, both in the relay events.

That was the end of Amy's Olympic career and her time spent swimming regularly. But she kept herself busy in retirement, working as a radio broadcaster, doing NFL sideline reporting, acting, and coaching. She and her husband also loved driving ATVs, and in June 2014, she suffered a serious spinal injury and a traumatic brain injury in an accident in Arizona. Amy was paralyzed from the waist down, and she remained in Arizona for medical care until she stabilized. Then she was airlifted to a hospital in Colorado, where she spent another eight weeks learning how to adapt to her new life in a wheelchair.

It would have been a difficult, painful summer for anyone, but for Amy, being so physically limited was especially confusing. After all, she'd been one of the world's top athletes, and she was still, at 41, accustomed to leading an active life. As Amy recovered, she decided she did not intend to change that. While at the hospital in Denver, Amy began intense rehab, hoping to walk again in some way. She worked with occupational therapists, who helped her learn the tricks of doing daily tasks from a wheelchair, physical therapists, and speech therapists, who helped her remember the words she'd struggled to recall due to her head injury. At one point, Amy took her rehab exercises to the pool, where on one hand, she realized she wasn't being challenged enough. Swimming still came naturally. On the other hand, though, it was the most difficult form of rehab, because she felt so different from the way she had at the peak of her career. "A lot of people who are injured say that getting in the swimming pool is liberating and free for them," Amy told NBC. "For me, that's where I feel the most paralyzed."

Two months into her stay in Denver, Amy was able to lift herself out of her wheelchair for the first time, taking steps with the help of a walker and a medical device that helped aid her movement. "Here it is . . . I'm WALKING!!! #onestepatatime #itcouldhappen," she wrote on Instagram. She said her rehab reminded her of training for

"IT'S NOT ALL RAINBOWS AND UNICORNS. BUT FOR ME IT'S NOT AN OPTION TO HAVE A BAD ATTITUDE."

the Olympics, and it kept her upbeat. "If you laugh and smile," she said, "it comes true, it happens." In the years since those steps, Amy has gotten back into sports, just in a new way. Her legs still can't carry her the way they used to, but she's worked on improving her upper body strength to compensate. She fell in love with adaptive CrossFit, which she first learned about while still in the hospital in Denver—and she's proven she's just as much of a star on land as in the pool. CrossFit is intense interval training, and in adaptive CrossFit, equipment is modified for each athlete's needs.

In July 2019, Amy competed for the first time since the Olympics. After months of intense CrossFit training—weight lifting, pull-ups, reps on the ski machine—she felt like an athlete again, with callouses on her hands from the barbells and the strong desire to compete. In the 2019 WheelWOD Games, she participated in the seated division against differently abled CrossFit athletes from all over the world, doing everything from burpees and swimming to distance throws and weightlifting. She took second place, the equivalent of a silver medal, just five years after her life turned upside down.

Amy has spent time in the pool since those initial days after the injury, using her muscular upper body to propel her body through the water. But now she's turning heads on land and in the gym, as much of an athlete as she was when she stood on the podiums six times in Atlanta and Athens. "You know, when they say, 'You'll never be able?'" Amy told MileHighSports.com. "No. That's again a hurdle or a wall that you're going to either go over or around or break under it or do whatever to get through it. For people who are wondering if they can, stop wondering and get out there and do it."

Becky Hammon

LEARN FROM THE BEST

In 2013, when Becky Hammon was 36 years old and playing in the first game of her 15th season in the WNBA, she tore her ACL. The knee injury was devastating. Becky played only 12 minutes that year, and she knew she was nearing the end of her career. It could have been frustrating to have trained all off-season and to know she wouldn't even be able to compete in a full game—and it *was* frustrating in some moments, especially to see her team, always a playoff contender, finish with a 12–22 record. Becky's team, the Silver Stars, shared an owner and a gym with the NBA team the Spurs. As Becky rehabbed at the teams' shared facilities, she began to form a deep connection with the coaches and players of the Spurs.

Becky had played in San Antonio for six years by then, and the Spurs roster had barely turned over. It featured some of the best players in the NBA, as well as one of the league's most respected coaches, Gregg Popovich. He and Becky hit it off. Actually, they'd first had a long conversation on a flight back from the 2012 Olympics in London, but when Becky was hurt, she and Popovich turned her time off into an opportunity. While Becky rehabbed, she interned with the Spurs, learning the ropes of coaching, and helping at practices and in the film room, where coaches and players watch video of past games and future opponents and break down the best ways to win. "What works on a team with girls works on a team with guys," she told *Sports Illustrated* in 2014. "Pick-and-rolls, reading defenses, scheming defenses—it's all similar. It's basketball."

Becky returned to the court for the Silver Stars in 2014, playing in 34 games as a point guard with the same dedication and work ethic that had marked the past two decades of her career. Never the biggest or fastest on the court—Becky stands just 5'6"—she still outworked and outsmarted opponents. "My game was never really about super-athleticism or speed, but it did evolve as I got older," she said in that same *Sports Illustrated* interview. "I got craftier. I began to see things and became great at making split-second decisions. I learned to use angles differently and understand footwork. I learned how to attack defenses better. I think I became better and quicker."

Becky knew the 2014 season would be her last in uniform. She thought back to her internship with the Spurs the year before, and both she and Popovich wanted to continue to work together. So they did. Before Becky's final season ended, she and the Spurs made an announcement: The point guard would be joining the team's coaching staff in the fall, making her the first woman to work as a full-time assistant coach in the NBA. (One woman, Lisa Boyer, had previously worked on an NBA staff, but only part-time.) Since Becky's coaching debut, 12 more women have sat on NBA benches.

As a coach, Becky has earned respect across the NBA, and many players have spoken out about her abilities on the bench. Though there's still never been a woman head coach in the league, Becky's path makes that outcome seem more likely. In San Antonio, she has served as the Spurs' summer league team coach, and she was the first woman in the NBA to hold that title. At summer league, Becky worked with the team's recent draft picks and other young players hoping to make the team, teaching them fundamentals and helping them make the jump to the high level of play in the NBA. Becky was also a coach during the 2016 NBA All-Star Game, this time getting a chance to coach some of the biggest names in the game.

Working for Popovich, Becky has been able to learn from one of the smartest minds in the NBA, and though Popovich is considered intimidating by many players, Becky has learned to stand up to him and voice her opinion in rooms where she's the only woman. "What I love about him is his world perspective," Becky told ESPN about her boss. "He always has a great way of breaking things down. It doesn't matter who he's talking to. He could be talking to a group of kindergartners and he's going to break it down to where they can understand it." Through hundreds of meetings, conversations, and dinners, Becky has absorbed the way Popovich thinks about the game, learning the minor differences between the men's game and the women's. And in December 2020, she got to put all that knowledge to the test when she took over as the Spurs acting head coach after Popovich was ejected, becoming the first woman in NBA history to take on that role.

"HOW DO YOU GET MORE CONFIDENT AT THE FREE THROW LINE? WELL, YOU GO AND SHOOT 100 FREE THROWS. YOU MISS, YOU GO BACK TO THE FREE THROW LINE, AND **YOU SHOOT 100 MORE.**"

Coco Gauff

NEVER STOP BEING **IN AWE**

Coco Gauff's tennis career got off to an early start. She began playing the sport when she was just six years old, inspired by watching Serena Williams's (see page 56) victory in the 2009 Australian Open. Like Serena, Coco is African American, and the older player was the ideal role model. It didn't hurt that tennis was an individual sport, which Coco preferred over team activities.

By the time she was eight years old, Coco was set on being a star on the court, and as the daughter of two athletes (her dad played basketball, her mother participated in track and field), she had the genetics to do well. Coco was just 13 when she made her Australian Open debut and 14 when she first appeared at the U.S. Open in New York. She became a household name soon after turning 15 in 2019, when she qualified for Wimbledon and began to win, and win, and win again. At Wimbledon, she defeated one of her idols, Venus Williams, in the first round in straight sets, making her the tournament's most exciting story. "When I first found out the draws came out, and I saw I was playing Venus, I felt like I was staring at the screen for a good 20 minutes, just thinking, *how is this real*?" Coco said on the "Winging It" podcast. "I've been thinking about his moment my whole life. I think I first watched her play when I was eight. . . . and then when I got on the court, I remember I put my music on full volume because I didn't want to hear the crowd."

Coco was successful again at the U.S. Open a few months later, until she lost to Naomi Osaka (see page 80), the top-ranked player in the world. She'd next face Osaka on a major stage in January 2020 in the third round of the Australian Open. There, she made it all the way to the semifinals of the doubles tournament. In the singles event, when she drew Osaka, the more experienced player was ranked No. 4 in the world. It was poised to be one of the best matches of the tournament, but instead, Coco destroyed Osaka in straight sets, never giving her opponent the advantage. After the victory, Coco paused mid-court for a post-match interview, which was broadcast through the speakers to the amazed crowd. Coco had just become the youngest person to defeat a top 5 player since Jennifer Capriati took down Gabriela Sabatini in 1991 at the U.S. Open, and to introduce the star, the interviewer pointed out that she was only 15 years old. The crowd roared. Coco, a high school sophomore, smiled and wiped sweat from her forehead, shielding herself from the cheers for just a moment and displaying a hot pink manicure. "What is my life?" Coco said. "Oh my gosh. Two years ago, I lost [in the] first round in juniors, and now I'm here. This is crazy."

Coco ended up losing in the Australian Open's fourth round, but even so, she made history down under. Then she moved on. She had to finish her homework, after all. Coco said during the tournament

"FOR ME, THE **DEFINITION OF AN ATHLETE** IS SOMEONE WHO ON THE COURT TREATS YOU LIKE YOUR WORST ENEMY, BUT OFF THE COURT CAN BE YOUR BEST FRIEND."

that her teachers at her online school gave her some extra time "considering the circumstances" and were allowing her to submit some assignments late. But once yet another major tournament was behind her, Coco had to get back to the responsibilities no older players face: reading, writing, and math. She's still a teenager who loves YouTube makeup tutorials, stresses about social media, and tries her best to attend as many of her younger brother's baseball games as possible.

Part of the reason Coco is able to excel at such a young age comes from her ability to focus. She's known around the sport for being able to remain calm after bad calls or difficult stretches during matches. But that's only half of the equation. Coco is also high-energy, fast, and coordinated, making tennis the perfect sport for her skill set. That she's been so successful comes as no surprise—though the wins and the fame have  come faster than many imagined. In early 2019, Coco was ranked No. 685. By 2020 she was up to No. 67, leapfrogging more than 600 talented women in the process. Sidelined by the pandemic just as she was starting to soar, Coco got off to a strong restart, reaching a ranking of 25 by early 2021, earning her first Grand Slam seeding in the French Open.

Still, Coco seems in awe of where she is: on the world's most famous courts, with thousands of fans cheering every point, every set, every win, and every time she opens her mouth.

LEARN MORE!

BOOKS AND BOOK SERIES

Breakaway by Alex Morgan (Simon & Schuster Books for Young Readers, 2017).

Epic Athletes series by Dan Wetzel (Henry Holt and Co.).

Flying High: The Story of Gymnastics Champion Simone Biles by Michelle Meadows (Henry Holt and Co., 2020).

Grace, Gold, and Glory by Gabrielle Douglas and Michelle Buford (HarperCollins, 2012).

In My Skin by Brittney Griner (Dey Street Books, 2015).

The Incredible Women of the All-American Girls Professional Baseball League by Anik Orrock (Chronicle Books, 2020).

Legends in Sports series by Matt Christopher (Little, Brown Books for Young Readers).

Life in Motion by Misty Copeland (Aladdin Young Readers, 2016).

My Shot by Elena Delle Donne (Simon & Schuster Books for Young Readers, 2018).

Rising Above: Inspiring Women in Sports by Gregory Zuckerman (Puffin Books, 2019).

She Persisted in Sports: American Olympians Who Changed the Game by Chelsea Clinton (Philomel Books, 2020).

Soul Surfer by Bethany Hamilton (MTV Books, 2016).

Strong by Kara Goucher (Blue Star Press, 2018).

Throw Like a Girl by Jenne Finch (Triumph Books, 2011).

Wolfpack by Abby Wambach (Celadon Books, 2019).

Women in Sports by Rachel Ignotofsky (Ten Speed Press, 2017)

WEBSITES

fierceathlete.org
hearhersports.com
iplaylikeagirl.org
lpga.com
ncaa.com
nwhl.zone
nwslsoccer.com
olympics.org
usagym.org
usfigureskating.org
usskiandsnowboard.org
womenssportsfoundation.org
wnba.com
wtatennis.com
xgames.com

YOUTUBE CHANNELS

NCAA Championships
The Norris Nuts
Olympics
U.S. Soccer
World Surf League
X Games

TED TALKS

Look for TED and TEDx Talks by:
- Aimee Mullins
- Amy Cuddy
- Billie Jean King
- Caroline Casey
- John Wooden
- Minda Dentler
- Stacy Sims

Generation Girl books celebrate amazing women who've been there, done that, and learned some valuable lessons along the way. Be inspired by their stories, learn from their struggles and successes, and get ready to change the world. Look for more hard-won wisdom in:

GIRL ACTIVIST

GIRL CEO
Priceless advice from trailblazing women

GIRL GENIUS
Bold breakthroughs from women in science